SHORT BACK AND SIGHS

SHORT BACK AND SIGHS continues the life of Margaret Rose Astbury, known to us all as Meg Hutchinson. Her childhood years was previously recalled in A PENNY DIP, however all childhoods end, and Meg's was no exception. It is often said 'a spoonful of sugar helps the medicine go down.' But not always! Within a few short years of leaving school she was to learn – as had her mother before her – the bitterness of 'medicine' can last half a lifetime.

SHORT BACK AND SIGHS

SHORT BACK AND SIGHS

by

Meg Hutchinson

Magna Large Print Books
Long Preston, North Yorkshire,
BD23 4ND, England.

British Library Cataloguing in Publication Data.

Hutchinson, Meg
    Short back and sighs.

    A catalogue record of this book is
    available from the British Library

    ISBN   978-0-7505-3564-9

Published in Large Print 2012 by arrangement with
Margaret Hutchinson Ltd.,
care of Judith Murdoch Literary Agency

Magna Large Print is an imprint of Library Magna Books Ltd.

Printed and bound in Great Britain by
T.J. (International) Ltd., Cornwall, PL28 8RW

In 'A Penny Dip' I write of experiences of growing up in the 'Black Country'. Though Wednesbury was a town of heavy industry, of iron and steel smelting it was – at least for us kids – not all doom and gloom, we found plenty of opportunities for mischief and played each to its full measure.

But all childhoods end, mine being no exception.

It is often said 'a spoonful of sugar helps the medicine go down'. But not always!

Within a few short years of leaving school I was to learn – as had my mother before me – the bitterness of 'medicine' can last half a lifetime.

CHAPTER ONE

'Margaret Astbury, she will never do any good, she will never amount to anything.'

What a boost to the morale of any young person leaving school! Yet that was the accidentally overheard hole in the corner conversation of a headmistress and a teacher colleague. The condemnation of a fourteen year old girl she had known for a little over six months but which seemed destined to affect my life for many years.

August Nineteen Forty Eight. At last freedom from the depressing and oppressive final months of what is usually referred to as the happiest years of your life; so they had been until the arrival of Miss Jones who was to take the place of a much loved and highly respected head Miss Harris. Making her debut to the 'leavers' class Miss Jones announced imperiously that the school she was *'leaving in order to take up this position is the school Princess Margaret attends.'* A faux pas! Not in her eyes, she obviously thought the children of the working classes in the smoke

11

clouded soot enshrouded Black Country town of Wednesbury would not have knowledge of the Princess being educated at Buckingham Palace and Windsor Castle; my answer enlightening her set the seal on her appreciation of me. I did not at that moment, nor in all the days which followed, exactly meet with that woman's approval; you could say 'flavour of the month' where I was concerned was never sweeter than lemon juice and bitter aloes.

Leaving school did not entirely prove the dream my young mind had nurtured. What I had not realised in those carefree days of childhood was that one day they would end as indeed they did. Margaret was put to working for her keep! Days which had been nine in the morning until four thirty in the afternoon now became nine in the morning until six in the evening. Not so very different you might say, but then the loss of school breaks of fifteen minutes morning and afternoon, a two hour lunch break (imposed during war time to offset the longer school day period which allowed mothers that extra time in their chosen line of war work), did in effect constitute quite a considerable difference.

The first encounter with the world of work was in a small drapery shop.

Appleyards of Darlaston standing on the corner of King Street and Pinfold Street sold, with the exception of shoes, coats and men's suits, every item of clothing and haberdashery needed from neck to toes. A wonderful Aladdin's cave of baby, children's and adult clothing, bibs and bodices, petticoats and pinafores, cottons and corsets, buttons, ribbons, knitting wool, knicker elastic and the sometimes vital to modesty safety pin.

One of the few customers I, as the youngest and most recently engaged sales girl, was allowed to serve came in asking for 'a pair o' bloomers please cock.' No problem. I was familiar with bloomers, mother wore them, long legs caught with elastic above the knee, and the term 'cock' was (and is) a widely used friendly address as maybe 'luv' in other parts of the country. So as I said, no problem. That is until I went into the back part of the shop to fetch the required item. Large deep drawers each neatly adorned with fancy metal card holders, the labels they held precisely and clearly printed with the contents of each seemed to reach almost to the ceiling. Ladies vests, ladies slips, ladies nightdresses, ladies hosiery cotton, ladies hosiery lisle, everything except ladies bloomers. Perhaps in my haste I had overlooked the label. Check

13

again, and then again. But it was no use, ladies bloomers just were not part of the stock. Yet had not mother always bought hers at Appleyards? About to return to my position at the counter there to inform the customer the article she required was not to be had, I was asked of Miss Gwyneth Appleyard, she having come to the back room to collect a customer's order, 'what was I looking for?' On hearing the object of my search she merely sniffed, pointed to a drawer then walked back to her counter. Uninitiated into polite language of ladies undergarments I had not connected bloomers with 'ladies divideds.'

Nor was that the only unfamiliar experience facing me that day. There was the method of payment. Used only to the local general sell mostly everything 'Patty Longmore's' who took customers' money over the counter, placing it in a drawer then returning change the same way, or those shops sporting large cash registers where on pressing relevant keys the amount payable for purchases appeared by what when first encountering this, had seemed to us kids a veritable feat of magic. Neither of those methods for Appleyards. Money handed to me I looked about for the nearest till. No till! A drawer then as with Patty Longmore's general and grocery and Stokes fish and chip shop adjacent to it. No drawer! This was getting to be embarrassing, the customer anxious to be about the rest of her day mumbling about 'think as folk got naught better to do!'

Not wanting to be caught again at a loss my heart spoken prayer was answered when from the corner of my eye I saw at the next counter the assistant, a girl a few years older than myself and much more in tune with the customs employed, place money and bill in a metal tube like container then insert this into a shuttle which whisked it away overhead to the cashier's desk, from where a few moments later change and receipt were returned via the same method. Goods priced in pounds, shillings and pence were inevitably priced to leave one penny or half penny and often one farthing to be given as change from a purchase and just as inevitably, the customer was invited to take in exchange a packet of pins or a card of two shirt buttons or maybe that valuable safety pin. The old adage of 'look after the pennies and the pounds will take care of themselves' had obviously been a well instructed lesson in the Appleyard method of shopkeeping.

I realised very quickly that forty four hours

15

of every week given to making morning and afternoon tea, washing up, tidying drawers already tidied to perfection relieved only by the not so regular privilege of attending a customer and all for the princely sum of twenty two shillings and sixpence a week, was not for me. So, not unhappily the world of bibs and baby gowns, shirts and socks, petticoats and pinafores, corsets, collars and 'ladies divideds' gave way to a second foray into the adult workplace. This followed the pattern laid down by father and three older sisters: Hilda, Phoebe and Ann, who each were employed in various aspects of the steel industry, but Hilda who by this time had moved with her husband and son to the North East no longer worked outside of the home: and Joan, the youngest of the family was yet at school.

'Dovaston Marine Engineering.' Situated on Holyhead Road this small factory was within a few minutes' walk of fifty one Dangerfield Lane but a whole world apart from the draper's shop.

'Y'can start in the mornin'.' The owner Mister Dovaston, 'Dovey' as I soon learned he was referred to when not within hearing, a slightly portly man wearing a light brown

coat overall smiled at the hesitant young girl seeking employment. He had asked no questions as to former employment, maybe he was of the opinion did I not prove suited then I could go elsewhere; jobs were two a penny and there was a ready supply of folk to take them.

So next morning, green heavy cotton overall in place, Margaret presented herself at the tiny office.

'You the new wench?' A man seemingly in his late twenties early thirties called from the doorway of the factory.

'*Won't be nobody there 'til nine,*' he called again, '*so if you're the wench gaffer said was to start this mornin' then y'best come on in.*'

Thus was my introduction into a complex, varied, often demanding yet never boring realm of industry.

It was Norman Phipps, tool setter cum all else who along with Doris, a middle aged machinist was the only other individual in the factory; the office being manned by Margaret, a dark haired, pleasant smiling woman of indeterminate age.

'Marine Engineering?' Didn't 'Marine' allude to ships? But with ships went the sea, yet nowhere in the country was further from the sea than Wednesbury, a Black Country

17

town in the very heart of the industrial Midlands! But then Wednesbury was very well connected if not with the majesty of the sea then with the 'cut', an interconnecting system of canals threading all of England, and canals were consistently used by narrowboats carrying the produce of steel mills and factories to sea ports or destinations inland. Narrowboats then had to be what this factory made. But as with 'Ladies Divideds', cash drawer or till, I could see no trace of boats.

Why then 'Marine Engineering'? The mystery was eventually solved by Norman.

'C'mon, I'll show you,' he said when at last I asked.

He had seen the frown of enquiry flash many times around the workshop during that first week and though doubtless having been asked that question on former occasions teasingly pretended not to know the reason for my confusion.

The machine I operated, a Ward 3A Capstan, being furthest from the end of the workshop and as a consequence shrouded in shadow I had not observed a large shape part covered by a sheet of tarpaulin.

'What is it?' I stared at the object held on wooden trestles, the body of it towering

above me.

'*That's the gaffer's pride an' joy*,' Norman laughed, '*or it will be should it ever get finished.*'

The '*gaffer's pride and joy?*' A thirty seven foot sea going yacht being built from scratch mostly it must be said by Norman who between setting up machines ready for operation, and sharpening worn tools, replacing broken ones, bringing in steel bars from the yard to feed machines making nuts, bolts and rivets, replacing or repairing fan belts together with a sundry other duties, worked on the yacht, assisted at odd times by the proud owner.

Was it ever finished? Yes. Some years later. I took mother in her wheelchair to see its removal from the factory. News of this had created a deal of interest in the immediate area, it being necessary to tear down the rear wall of the factory building in order for the crane to lift the boat free and deposit it onto a large low loader lorry. I have over the years often wondered what name was given 'Dovey's pride and joy', maybe someone might be able to tell me.

It had been a year or so previous to my leaving school Hilda's brother-in-law Ralph

Hutchinson having received notice of conscription into the forces had written from County Durham could he and his brother whom he had not seen for some ten years possibly meet before he entered the Army? Where to stay was the real question, Hilda and Bill and baby son living at our parents' house along with three younger sisters. Three bedrooms, eight people, no room for a young man. That would have been a perfectly logical response. But possibly because of a life which at the best of times had never been easy, mother had learned the art of dodging logic. Her mantra had become 'things will work out if only you let them.' In other words, if you don't go looking for problems there will be less to solve. So Bill was given the reply his brother could stay with us.

Mother's decision made, no argument from father who for half a lifetime had shared with her the problems of rearing a family through years of dole queue and then of wartime, seeing how she had made a penny do the work of a shilling had complete faith this present dilemma would prove no insurmountable obstacle.

All well and good; but three bedrooms and now nine people ... the classic quart in a pint pot syndrome! Mother's remedy? Simple ...

you first remove some of the contents of the pot. So it was arranged that for one week, sixteen year old Ann and ten year old Joan would sleep in the front room of the house which Phoebe rented part of while thirteen year old Margaret would stay home sharing a bedroom with Hilda and year old Paul, thus leaving a bedroom for Bill to share with his brother.

The week went well enough, Ralph taking to the family like a duck to water, and he didn't seem to mind a schoolgirl being roped in to make a foursome on a couple of visits to the cinema; this after meeting his arrival at Birmingham New Street railway station I had curtly told him if he didn't like what he saw, 'you know what you can do!'

With his departure I and probably the rest of the family thought we would see no more of the pleasant young man, but as is so often the case, things do not always go the way it is expected. During the weeks of training weekend passes were frequently granted and each of these were matched with the request could Ralph Hutchinson visit again to Dangerfield Lane? Mother already seeing in him the son she never had did not hesitate in saying yes.

As on that first visit it was myself accompanied Hilda, Bill and his brother on visits to the cinema, we went with them to see him off back to camp from Wednesbury's White Horse bus terminal. It was during one of these goodbyes, the two of us standing a little apart from Hilda and Bill, he asked would I write to him? Certain mother would not object I agreed. 'Did I have something I would give him for a keepsake?' This second question was not so easily answered. I had no jewellery, no personal item other than a small comb in a dark green leather case. Would that suffice as a parting gift? Yes. He smiled, slipped the paltry gift into the pocket of his tunic and stepped onto the bus.

Then came one more letter to mother. Embarkation for Greece was to take place shortly, could a few days of the leave permitted be once again spent with her family? Now this request, if not a surprise to mother was certainly that for me. Ralph had learned on that last occasion of his spending a weekend with us his brother had taken wife and son and returned to the family home at Birtley, County Durham. Why then when grounds for that first visit had been a reunion between brothers did he not go home, spend that last week with father and brother? But again mother agreed and with Ann, Margaret and Joan sharing a bedroom Ralph once again spent the week at fifty one Dangerfield Lane. Puzzling as was this latest request to visit, even more puzzling still was that each time he came it was the company of myself he seemed to prefer; of his newly found 'sisters' it was myself he would escort to school, me he would wait for in the playground in order we might walk home together, me he laughed with but didn't tease.

That week followed the pattern of every other visit, all that is for one evening at the cinema. Ralph and I had gone to the Regal in Darlaston to see the film 'Seven Brides for Seven Brothers', sat in the posh seats of the balcony, a most unusual treat for a young girl used to the locally termed 'spitters' ... the cheapest seats situated at the front of the auditorium from which you emerged with a painful neck caused by craning the head backward in order to look up at the screen. Ralph rested his hand over mine covering both with his Army beret. The first time in all those meetings he had touched me and it would happen just once more in many, many months. Nothing was said between us, I think I saw his holding my hand as a big brother gesture, certainly no more than that for didn't the local lads of eighteen ignore thirteen year old 'kids'; why then would I view that touch in the cinema as anything other than 'brotherly'?

Soon then it was Saturday, the day Ralph must return to camp. Could I see him off, this time not from the White Horse at Wednesbury but from Birmingham New Street, that same railway station in which we first met? The train was leaving at three o'clock in the afternoon, I could be back home by four. Now a competent fourteen year old I was given permission, mother saying she saw no reason I shouldn't 'see the lad off.'

The bus journey to Birmingham was a one sided affair, me chattering on as usual but Ralph barely saying a word. Then on the platform of the busy station it was three o'clock and true to time the train gathered steam, a guard calling 'all aboard.'

The smile I had come to know as being especially for me, a quiet deep in the eyes smile so different from the laughing smile shared with my sisters, reflecting from grey blue eyes he took my hand. *'This is not goodbye,'* he murmured quietly. Then before I was aware he unpinned the brooch from my lapel, a heart and key pendant linked by a short length of chain. It had cost only a shilling or so from Woolworths but even so I was far from pleased when he snapped the chain separating the two pieces. About to make this fact very evident I was stopped by the look in those eyes, a look which seemed to be storing every part of me within them. The guard called again, a warning shout of the train's imminent departure and as it echoed along the platform Ralph enclosed the heart shaped half of the pendant in his hand and returning the key to me said softly, *'you are one part, I am the other, one day we will join the two together.'*

That shilling or so pendant even though broken became and remains a very treasured possession.

CHAPTER TWO

Despite everything about factory work being different to the position of shop assistant, overalls grease stained an hour after starting work on Monday morning, the loud noise of machinery, the mixing of 'suds' ... machine oil and water used to lubricate cutting tools ... the water fetched in a bucket from a standpoint in the men's toilets... I thought this practice would be one more task assigned to Norman but though his answer was a smiling 'you fetch your own', I was not deterred. Those last few months of school, the few spent in the drapery shop were forgotten. I was happy in my factory job. Even carrying a bucket filled with water presented no problem, but how to be sure that toilet was not occupied? Norman was the only male in the workshop, a quick glance showed any absence on his part, but what of 'Dovey', and of course any visitor to the factory? I could see only one solution ... sing. How many times did I do that when approaching that 'prohibited' building, how many times giving a concert all my own while waiting for that bucket to fill; a glede under a door it might have sounded and certainly it was no operatic rendering but it prevented a situation which without this warning, could have proved embarrassing.

The hours too were different to those worked previously. Work at 'Dovastons' beginning an hour sooner making a working day of nine hours. This for five days combined with four hours on Saturday morning completed a working week of forty nine rather than the former forty four served at the draper's shop. But that was more than recompensed by the friendly attitude of everyone, there was no hierarchy, the youngest most recently employed being treated in exactly the same fashion as the long established. All that was except in the matter of pay. The practice of paying less to workers under twenty one years of age than was paid to those having paced that landmark had long been observed as was that of paying women less than men even though employed on the same or comparable jobs. But where was the fairness in that I asked myself upon learning Doris was being paid one penny three farthings for the cast iron pulleys she machined where I, doing exactly the same job, producing an equal number of finished product was paid just three farthings. Yes she had been employed at the firm longer than myself, yes she was older than myself but in this particular case it could not be claimed she was more adept or more skilled, so where the justification in so different a pay scale?

'It'll make no odds you complainin', the gaffer *won't pay no more'*, was Norman's verdict upon my line of reasoning, and though sympathetic and understanding of my grievance, Doris was of the same opinion. *'You'll be paid no more.'* Perhaps not, perhaps doing an 'Oli-

ver' and asking 'please sir I want some more' would result in my being given my cards and told to leave, but feeling as I did the injustice of the situation I asked anyway. Taken aback by the enterprise of a fifteen year old demanding equality of pay for equality of labour? Or amused at the audacity of it? I can't say, but payment for each finished pulley was increased to a penny farthing.

Father shook his head at such folly as risking the 'sack' but mother was highly delighted when Friday evening's pay packet revealed three pounds and several pence. I also was delighted. Pocket money of one pound was a great deal more acceptable than had been two shillings and sixpence.

Life was proving changed indeed and not just in the workplace but also at home. Unlike school days when most of those hours free of the classroom – and from air raid shelters – were spent playing with friends – now a number of those hours had to be given to helping in the home. Leaving the factory at noon on Saturday my first task was to scrub my overall, that was a task each sister had to do for herself, mother did all of the laundry but never washed overalls. This scrubbed then and put to dry it was turn out the living room; polish, sweep, black lead the fireplace and clean the windows. Joan excused duties because of being still at school, Hilda no longer living at home, Phoebe now with a place shared with her husband, it was Ann and I completed these tasks between us before we were free to do the girly things.

Saturday evenings were looked forward to with great anticipation, but they needed to be prepared for and in the Astbury household this took almost as long, and could prove equally strenuous as going to work.

It would start with a spoonful of sugar. This being rationed had mother warn, 'remember, what y' mixes with that water y' don't get in your tea!' But despite any reminder the sugar was dissolved in a cup of hot water. The solution combed through the hair a strand at a time before winding onto a metal 'Dinkie' curling pin had it set rock hard; but never mind, the curls it produced would last all evening. Next it would be out with the frock or the skirt and blouse to be ironed for the evening jaunt to Darlaston Town Hall's weekly dance. Now ironing was something to be reckoned with. Flat iron heated before the fire or on the ring of the gas stove had in the Astbury household given

way to the new fangled electric iron mother
had been prevailed upon to buy from the
travelling salesman carrying samples of
wares in his pack, so 'Packman'. In my area
of the Black Country this term was soon
reduced to 'Packy.' But there were no sockets
in the wall, no three pin plugs, these had not
been installed in the council built houses of
Dangerfield Lane, so the only method by
which this miracle of science could be used
was by removing the bulb from the ceiling
light and plug the flex from the iron into the
fitting; with no safety cut out it can only be
providence kept us from being fried! But we
never gave a thought to the possibility of
risk, this was progress and we girls revelled
in it. Progress though had not yet developed
to the point where nylon stockings, presum-
ing you were fortunate enough to find any,
had not yet become a cheap commodity. The
one pair I had been allowed to purchase
during my time at Appleyards had cost
fourteen shillings and eleven pence and with
receiving only two shillings and sixpence
weekly pocket money, it was dad stumped
up the remainder. So nylons being rarer than
boobs on a fish, pure silk just as expensive,
then you had the choice of lisle, a little less
costly or the even cheaper cotton. Ugh! Both

thick as paint they were thought alright for mother but for her daughters the retort, 'I wouldn't be seen dead in them!' adequately sums their reception.

But legs, especially for the Saturday dance, had to look their best and bare legs not being in vogue then a substitution needed to be found. The cliché which speaks of necessity being the mother of invention proving once more to be true it was, after soaking an hour in the bath, providing of course there was a coal fire to heat the water or money enough for the gas meter to heat water in the wash boiler, which was not always so and in the event meaning a flannel and a kettleful of water in the washing up bowl; but frustrating as that frequently was, the preliminaries went on regardless. So rubbed and scrubbed till the skin tingled, a head full of dreams of the pleasures of the dance it was time to tackle the problem of what to do about the legs. They must somehow appear to be sheathed in the sheerest of stockings, but how to do that without nylons? Enter the 'mother of invention'.

Once again water provided the answer but this time without the sugar. A small amount of water carried in a saucer to the back garden and there mixed with sand until it became a sludgy paste you had the ingredients, then with a couple of housebricks providing a footrest, skirts tucked into knicker legs it was on with sand. Daubed, courtesy of your best friend, toe to hip, you returning the favour while waiting for your own application to dry, it remained only to brush the dried residue of sand away, this leaving a trace of golden brown worthy of a week in the Riviera sunshine. Adding to this a line drawn from ankle to bottom with a black eyebrow pencil you had legs Betty Grable might envy. Yes, sanding the legs did have a side effect. If like myself, you arrived home too tired after a night of quick step and foxtrot to wash away all trace of sand before climbing into bed, you discovered evidence of it next morning all over the sheets. Lord, the times mother almost suffered a coronary over that!

So legs finished with a sexy seam it was the turn of the face. A smear of 'Pond's Cold Cream', a powder puff loaded with 'Tokalon' face powder to drown the freckles, a touch of rouge or lipstick smoothed over the cheeks providing a demure blush, a smear of 'Vaseline' darkened with a fingertip of soot from the chimney carefully added to the eyelashes it remained only to apply the favourite 'Tangee' lipstick for the transformation to be complete. So with the dress which had been ironed until not the least semblance of crease dare show itself, a dab of 'Evening in Paris' perfume behind the ears Cinderella was off to the ball.

Saturday evening was a pleasure but not the sole provider. There were the cinemas and now with one pound pocket money, enough could be set aside from clothes and sundries I must now pay for myself, to visit the Regal or the PictureDrome, not the Olympia for by this time the locally termed 'Limp' had become a little too down market for the young and trendy, but either way the intention was enjoyment and I got plenty of that with lads spinning a line and my blasé heard it all before attitude hiding the satisfaction this attention afforded.

That evening over and done, Ann and I were once again engaged in cleaning house, Sunday morning seeing bedrooms scrubbed and dusted. Sheets and pillow cases waited until Mondays when they were washed and somehow, despite winter rain and snow, had to be dried and replaced on the beds, the restrictions of wartime as well as of household cash as yet still in operation.

Sunday lunch was a reverent institution in our house. Even the bleak times of the thirties with hardly a penny remaining of dad's labour pay mother would manage to find a potato and maybe a swede and even though there was often no meat to grace the plate, the seven of us would sit down together thankful, especially during later times when bombing raids were heavy, and thank God for what we had.

But it was after lunch with dad snoozing and mother often in the yard gossiping with neighbours or as sometimes visiting the cemetery to place flowers on the grave of her parents, the shenanigans of the previous afternoon began all over again.

Though bound by strictures still ruling the Sabbath with a pretty strong grip, there were a few exceptions which with careful manipulation could be overcome. One such was Sunday opening of cinemas. Regulation to one showing, four o'clock in the afternoon until seven thirty in the evening and allowing entry only for those over the age of sixteen. This very new treat introduced after the end of the war was a beckoning finger I could not resist. So, 'dressed to death and killed with fashion' one Sunday say Mary Butler, she seventeen, and me, two years her junior, off to the 'pictures'. Not the Regal or the PictureDrome for in either of those establishments despite the over effusive use of powder and lipstick, we might possibly be recognised. So turning our backs on Darlaston it was take the bus to Wednesbury and the Gaumont.

Almost to the Box Office confidence fading I pushed several coins into Mary's hands trying to sound very nonchalant when saying, *'you get the tickets.'*

'Two one and sixes please.' Pushing forward the three shillings which would allow us seats in mid auditorium, the rear seats costing one shilling and ninepence and the balcony an unthinkable two shillings and sixpence, Mary smiled.

''Ow old am you?' Inside the glass fronted kiosk the cashier looked questioningly at Mary.

'I'm seventeen,' Mary replied truthfully.

'Oh ar,' the cashier sniffed scornfully, *'an' my arse be a lemon!'* With that her glance switched to me standing at Mary's shoulder. *'Yoh be old enough'*, she said tartly, *'yoh can go in but this one don't be gettin' no ticket!'*

Being turned away was all the more surprising seeing we had several times pulled the same trick while I was fourteen, powder and paint being plastered on after leaving the house and vigorously washed off before

35

returning. But the initial embarrassment of this encounter quickly fading we walked back to Dangerfield Lane giggling every step of the way.

CHAPTER THREE

Mid July and the annual two week industrial holiday was coloured by the prospect of my first experience of being away from home, though not entirely separated from the family for along with my cousin Mary Green who I had spent all of my, as yet, short life with, I was to spend two weeks in the North East with Hilda, her husband and young son and her father-in-law. This holiday was heaven from the start; green spacious fields instead of fields of factories; South Shields, Marsden and other seaside places havens of delight far removed from Wednesbury's streets of soot blackened buildings: and the fact of having no swimsuit in which to sunbathe presented no problem at all, a bra was as good as a bikini top would be once they hit the market.

The return journey to Birmingham was

not so enjoyable, stood in the corridor of a train packed so tightly with bodies it could, as dad would have remarked, 'proved an object lesson to sardine canners.' Eight hours without sitting down for a moment was not all the problems involved with getting home. A bus brought us to the White Horse in Wednesbury but Dangerfield Lane was near enough two miles from there.

Eleven thirty at night, Holyhead Road dark and eerily empty we began to walk, struggling to carry over filled suitcases and myself in need of a wee. Need reached desperation point. To proceed would result in wet knickers and what would mother make of that! What she made of the fact of our returning home without informing her and thus being met at New Street Station I won't bother you with, except to say she bothered me with it for days after. So, Mary and I were on the way home and as I've told stopping every few yards so I could plait my legs against the threat of an inconsiderate bladder. It was drawing level with Saint James Street I made my decision. The school I had so recently left had toilets in the school yard. These you could not, even as a child fresh from the Infants department, have bribed me enough to have me visit them. Several cubicles faced by a high wall lined an earth floor, painfully narrow, open to the sky passageway, the toilets they contained consisting of wooden board with a hole at its centre, this open above a channel leading I knew not where, nor having any individual flushing system to convey waste there. Little wonder then when early in school life, presented with view of what with so many children using them was no pleasant sight, I would suffer any belly ache rather than enter one of what we had labelled, 'black hole of Calcutta.'

But many hours of a train journey whose corridors were so congested it would have been an impossibility to get a toilet even had I been so inclined as to risk encountering the same hygienic conditions as those of Saint James' School imposed their own condition. It was visit one of these cubicles now or face the wrath of mother. The contest conceded at the first throw, I left Mary with the suitcases and darted the few yards along Saint James' Street and into the school playground. Dark as ink the night seemed instantly to close in on me, the hulk of the building itself a blacker shape among deep shadows seeming to whisper insidiously, voices in the blackness murmuring 'never do any good ... never do any good...' This was just the tiny schoolyard, what fears then lurked in that lavatory block? Why hadn't I quickly lowered my knickers and taken a wee on the patch of waste ground adjacent to the yard? There was no one to witness the deed. But the idea not entering my head and my refusing even if it had, I was left with one course of action. Memory rather than vision leading the way, breath held against fear as well as odour I forced myself along, feeling along that high walled passage and into a toilet, the odour of which guided as efficiently as any torch.

The oh so much needed ablution accomplished it was profound relief as much as fear if those 'whispers' had me race back to where Mary waited with the suitcases. But relief turned to concern when I saw, standing one each side of her in the darkness, two tall figures. Heart thumping from this new fear I almost cried relief of a different kind when seeing the figures were those of uniformed policemen.

Hearing our tale of woe, how we had been forced to stand up all that distance from Newcastle upon Tyne and now were walking the rest of the way alone, they simply nodded, wished us goodnight and proceeded on their way toward the local police station. So much for protection! But then happily, those days did not so much require it.

But one short day following the holiday and it was back to the factory.

Situated close as 'Dovastons' was to the house meant I could take my dinner break at home and it was during one such dinner time mother said there was a letter for me. Having fulfilled the promise made to Hilda's brother-in-law to write to him, receiving only one letter in reply, this practice had gone by the board, so who was writing to me? The answer was no one, well no one writing; the envelope contained a photograph of Ralph in summer khaki uniform of lightweight trousers, cotton tunic open at the throat, sleeves rolled above the elbow, beret casually held over one knee found a place on the shelf of the living room fireplace. He may not have written but then he had not entirely forgotten.

A little while after this, my cousin Mary Green who lived in Margaret Road just around the corner from Dangerfield Lane, came to say she had received a letter from John Pickard, a best friend of Ralph's she had become friendly with when she and I had spent those two weeks with Hilda in

Birtley. The letter included news of Ralph sailing for England. Very nice! I shrugged indifferently. But why tell me? Had he wished us to know of his return he would have put word of it in with the photo, but he hadn't, that then was proof enough he was no longer interested in his sister-in-law's family. But later in the week when mother's letter arrived that conclusion was seen to be misapprehension. The old request was being made again and as on every other occasion of asking the request was granted.

The day of arrival, saw the familiar procedure in place, three sisters sharing a bedroom with the one vacated made ready for the young man mother had grown so very fond of.

Our next door neighbour, Lucy Harris, a good friend whose one failing, if it could be called that, was she simply had to know everything going on in the Lane, so of course was well acquainted with news of that forthcoming event, and as usual found reason to be in our house around the time our visitor arrived. It was just mother and myself at home, father not yet back from work, Ann and Joan out with their friends. I had no reason to feel apprehensive, it was not like some total stranger was about to land himself on us, yet I was edgy, so much so that when Lucy, who had obviously been watching from her window, came rushing into the kitchen to say Ralph was just a few yards off, I took myself into the living room. What did I say to him? Would he be the same Ralph I had known before? Would he want to be bothered with that 'kid' of eighteen months ago? So what if no were the answer to the knot of questions rushing through my mind, that didn't mean I should feel nervous, yet unreasonably I did.

Moments later he was there in the kitchen. I heard him ask 'where is Margaret?' and the next second I was being swept into his arms and kissed. Not it seemed quite the Ralph of before, the one who had only briefly touched my hand; but the soft smile and the gentle eyes were those I had known. That week went much as the others he had spent with the family, he escorting mother a couple of afternoons to the cinema, mother's most favoured pastime, or on occasions accompanying her to Darlaston to carry the shopping, but in the evening at six o'clock he would be outside the factory waiting for me just as he had once waited in the school yard. The slight nervousness I had felt at his arrival fast disappeared, I was relaxed in his company and he, it appeared, had not lost his preference for mine. Apart from the inevitable cinema, he making no complaint of already having seen the film with mother, the evenings were mostly passed talking with mother and dad, but when mother's favourite radio programmes were due to start the two of us would go stand at the garden gate. Though alone, not once was there a single touch of the hand, not the merest peck to the cheek, that kiss given immediately on coming to the house had been nothing more than sheer exuberance at being demobbed, the greeting of a 'brother' for a 'sister.' It can be understood then my laugh when on the Thursday evening, stood as usual at the gate, he suddenly asked, *will you marry me?* Was he beginning to tease me the same way he teased my sisters? Was he joking with me as he so often joked with them? His quietly assuring this was not the case, that he meant what he had asked I tossed my head replying, *don't talk daft, I'm only fifteen!*

Teasing or not I presumed my tart response to put an end to it but the next evening, again outside of the house, he put the question again, *will you marry me?*

It is difficult after sixty years to describe the emotions of that moment. I had liked this man from ... almost ... the moment of being introduced to him on the platform of a railway station, strangely I had missed him the first time of his returning to his Army unit and did so on each subsequent departure, and certainly I had not forgotten him during his time spent abroad; now he was about to leave again and I was all mixed up. A girl so young could not possibly be in love, so why did I not want him to go? And why did I want so much to say yes to that proposal? But that was impossible, I was far too young to know my own mind! And now suddenly far too shy to say what was really in it so I took refuge in similar curt retort: *'don't talk daft, I've told you I'm only fifteen, how can I marry you!'*

The refusal of the previous evening had been met with silence and I expected this second to be met with the same, but as I turned to go inside he said equally quietly, *'you will marry me ... even if you have to!'*

A threat? From someone who had only twice touched my hand and once kissed my mouth? Maybe I should have thought it so but looking at his face, seeing the expression in his eyes, I felt no intimidation, no ominous sense of any kind, just an inward inexplicable quiet happiness. Then next day he was gone, and as with those months of National Service no letters addressed Miss Margaret Astbury and definitely none signed Ralph Hutchinson found their way to Fifty One Dangerfield Lane.

Mother's favourite visitor once more departed the household settled to its usual routine. If she had guessed anything of the feelings it seemed that young man held for me she made no reference to it, as for myself I clung to the idea those proposals had been one big tease, that of course they had not been intended to be seen as anything other than that, and the 'threat'? That too had been a joke, one I had misread and should forget; after all now demobbed and back with his family there was no more reason for us to ever meet again.

Days and nights no longer subject to the hazards of air raids, Darlaston's teenagers added a diversion to their agenda. Cinemas cost money, the dance halls likewise and pocket money having to account for all but room and board their visits to those pleasure domes must be restricted. But a stroll around the town centre cost nothing. This then became the regular Sunday evening pastime.

Always in groups, girls pretending indifference to wolf whistles but giggling delight when out of earshot, lads feigning no more than the same casual inattention the parade went on. King Street, Victoria Road to the park entrance and there turning to retrace their route the circuit, probably no more than half a mile in length, was walked over and over again. Harmless enough until one man, seemingly much older and always alone, began harassing girls making their way home. Was he maybe the same man I had noticed on one occasion at the Regal cinema move several times to a different seat? People sat next to him talking taking enjoyment from the film? I found out when a further choice of seat was next to mine. A couple of minutes and I felt a touch to my knee. An accidental brush! I shuffled hoping to dislodge it. But the tactic failed, the touch now becoming a slow upward stroke of my leg. Too scared to think properly I whispered to the friends I was with saying I couldn't see the screen clearly, then scrambled past them to sit the other side. The man moved again taking the seat I had vacated. Peace reigned, the film went on, me breathing more easily until with a shout that echoed throughout the auditorium, Jean Gough was on her feet pushing past startled patrons to reach the aisle, a bewildered Joan Potts and a not so bewildered Margaret Astbury following out of the cinema. Fright, Jean's cross accusations of 'you might have told me!' and my fibs of having no knowledge of what on earth the sudden exit had been all about dissolved into giggles at the ructions we must have caused. We should have reported the incident to the manager but as with an event which had happened three or four years earlier when my cousin Mary Green and me having a Sunday afternoon picnic beside the canal were approached by a man, my sensing all was not right I got hastily to my feet ready to run, but Mary was not so quick, she was grabbed by the man, he pushing his hand inside her knickers only releasing her when our terrified screams had the lads swimming in the canal come running, chasing him away. The feeling of somehow being myself to blame for this unfortunate encounter prevented my telling mother of what had occurred and it was something of that same self guilt had me keep a still tongue over the cinema affair.

Not so Ann.

The problem of the 'roving hand' took a different turn. The possibility of being assaulted, girls suddenly finding themselves faced with an unwelcome view of male anatomy or else being followed by a man calling unsavoury remarks had, Ann decided, to be brought into the open.

It came to light in the Astbury house when one evening Ann came rushing into the living room. Snatching up the iron poker from beside the fireplace uttering threats of bashing someone's head she was stopped from running out again by father. Demanding he be told what the matter was, hearing Ann and her friend had been followed from Darlaston subjected all the time to unpleasant remarks he took the poker from her. 'George!' Mother said anxiously reading his intent, 'George, don't go doin' anythin' hasty!' Already halfway through the door the answer drifted back. 'Oh I won't do anythin' hasty, I'll tek me time givin' that bugger a hidin'!'

He did not catch the culprit. Neither did anyone else so far as I recall, and though alleged or otherwise the incidents grew less, fear of them persisted. It was this fear led to the following episode.

The second eldest of mother's five daughters, Phoebe, had moved from the rooms she and her husband Andrew had rented in a house directly across the road from ours and now lived with baby son in a small back to back very old house in the Kings Hill area of Wednesbury. It was her practice most days to come see mother, and quite often again in the evening when her husband would accompany her, he then going to the pub with dad. But inevitably dad would return alone, Andrew knowing that no way would Phoebe be allowed to go home by herself simply leaving that to the family, the 'family' being dad. But one Saturday evening dad having gone with workmates on a coach outing was not available so it was Ann and myself would be the escort. Ann, it should be explained, was a past master in telling others what to do, organisation was a germ in her blood. That night was no exception. Giving precise instructions as to what I must do should we meet with Darlaston's 'Phantom Flasher' she picked up the bread knife tucking it beneath her coat sleeve. Nothing untoward taking place, Phoebe and toddler safely in the house, Ann and I set off for home. Walking back toward the Bull Stake, Ann caught my elbow. There, passing beneath a street light a man with coat collar turned up was coming toward us. This, Ann immediately decided, was the 'Flasher'. Hand tightening on my arm she hissed, 'now remember what I've told you, when he gets level with us you run and I'll stab him!'

Was it our hearts thumping or had the anti aircraft guns so often heard a few years ago begun pounding again?

'Get ready our Marg!' Ann hissed again the knife sliding down her sleeve into her hand. 'When I say run, you run!' Nearer came the figure, head tucked low on the chest, coat collar obscuring the face, hands thrust into pockets. Nearer ... still nearer. Fingers digging painfully into my arm, my throat so tight with fear to complain, Ann repeated her warning then distance between us and the oncoming threat no more than a step, she pushed me free at the same time raising the knife to strike ... it was in that very moment with a quiet laugh the figure said, 'Evenin' girls.' Father had ever been one for teasing us girls, often chuckling over a trick he played on us, but that night, returning home to discover Ann and I were taking Phoebe home and so coming to bring us back, his 'trick' almost proved one too many.

CHAPTER FOUR

The upheaval of war had in the main little effect on my life. Being a six year old when it began I, like Ann three years older and Joan three years younger, was bothered very little, myself wondering what all the fuss was about, why dig a huge hole in the garden then build it over with corrugated metal sheeting and garden soil? And why on earth leave a warm bed in the middle of the night and trundle into this eternally damp 'steel tent' to spend the rest of the night as I thought camping out? Of course as bombing raids intensified I soon learned the cause of these almost nightly migrations into the back garden, the associated inconvenience, discomfort and fear leaving me with a definite distaste for camping, an aversion which I hold to this day.

But in those first teen years with the conflict over and discomfort forgotten the world for me was rosy. A job I enjoyed, a huge hike in pocket money and parents who trusting to the creed by which they raised their children, namely treat others as you would have them treat you, placed few objections on the friends we made or how we spent our free time.

Dancing being top of the list of pleasures for each of five sisters it was a great treat for me when on occasions I and our cousin Mary Green were allowed to attend one under the watchful eye of Ann. This we did some half dozen times, then Mary's mother decided it had to end. Harmless as those evenings were, quite why my mother's sister made that decision I never did discover; but then Aunt Phoebe was not always the most logical of women. Her reasoning, knowing as she did the location of Woden youth club, could not have been the same as that of the headmistress newly appointed to Saint James' School.

As with that later overheard conversation in which it was stated, 'Margaret Astbury will never do any good, she will never amount to anything,' another deduction of Miss Jones was never learned of by mother.

The occurrence happened one morning. Having taken it upon herself to search the pockets of every coat in the cloakroom she discovered in mine a slip of paper on which was written, 'will you be going to the Woden tomorrow night?' Intending to pass the note to Mary during morning assembly the opportunity was lost when my late arrival had me rush to join the class already filing into the school hall, hence the paper remained in my pocket the question left to be asked during morning break.

But before break Mary, in the same class as myself, was sent for by the headmistress. In Miss Jones' study the slip of paper was produced.

'Will you please explain this!'

The demand snapping like a steel trap closing, Mary already nervous at the summons to that room answered tremblingly she had not seen it.

Glacier cold eyes watching for the merest indication of a lie, hailstone words rapped, 'I did not ask had you seen it, I asked you to explain!'

The paper pushed a little nearer Mary read again. 'It ... it says will you be going to the "Woden" tomorrow night?'

Never the most patient teacher this reply had the effect of waving a red rag before a bull. Snatching the paper back across the desk the headmistress fumed. 'I can read child, but you, it seems, cannot understand a simple sentence so I will ask again; explain the meaning of this note.'

Bewildered Mary sat silent. What was it she was being asked to say?

The silence broken by a loud irritated tut the interrogation began again.

'How often do you visit the "Woden"?'

The question one she could understand, Mary answered quickly. 'Not every Thursday, mum doesn't always let me go.'

Frostbitten the stare continued. 'I see. And when you are allowed to go, what time do you arrive there?'

'About seven o'clock.'

'And you stay how long?'

Truthful and quick as before Mary gave the reply. ''Til about ten.'

Triumph gleaming like icecaps in the Arctic the narrow face almost bore a smile. Assumption was proved correct. 'I see,' Miss Jones returned exultantly, 'and what exactly do you do while you are there?'

Once more there was no hesitation in Mary's answer, 'We dance.'

'Dance!' Anger signals flashed in the glance. Was the girl daring to be facetious?

As wary as were all of the students of this headmistress, wanting nothing more than to be out of that room away from the person none of us had any liking for, hoping this would satisfy Mary enlarged on her answer. 'They play music and we dance.'

Frost closed in even harder, the glare that of icicles. 'And where is this Woden?'

The answer had not satisfied. Perplexed as to where this was leading or just what it was all about Mary said, 'Darlaston Miss, in Franchise Street.'

Lips clamped, nostrils flaring to allow the passage of snatched breath the paper was set back on the desk. The reply obviously did not fit a firmly held hypothesis.

Dismissed with instruction to ask the class teacher send Margaret Astbury immediately to that room Mary scuttled thankfully out of it.

Used to being thought the culprit no matter the crime rebellion surged strong in me as I knocked on the door. Even so I knew better than to allow that emotion to get the upper hand for hell itself, never mind the awful Miss Jones, would know no anger to beat that of mother should reports of 'back answering' reach her ears.

The questions Mary later related had been put to her were put verbatim to me until reaching that which asked the location of the 'Woden.' That came not as 'Where is this Woden?' but as, 'The Woden, that is at the

High Bullen is it not?'

'No.' I answered. 'It isn't in Wednesbury, it's in Darlaston.'

'Where in Darlaston?'

Had this woman in some previous life been an officer of the Spanish Inquisition, or a member of the infamous Tudor Star Chamber? Was this how they had interrogated their unfortunate victims? Indignation threatening any moment to become mutiny I bit back a retort I knew would have repercussions when reported to mother so answered instead. 'Franchise Street. It's a club room belonging to the Woden Engineering Works, they provide it as a youth centre. Sometimes Mary and me are allowed to go there with my sister Ann.'

The pin that pricked the balloon, this reply saw the end of the questioning.

Why the cross examination?

'Woden' was not solely the title of a Darlaston Engineering firm, but was also, though at that time unknown to Mary and myself, attributed to a public house which still stands relatively close by Wednesbury High Bullen. It was this latter the headmistress had chosen to suspect the two of us visited on those Thursday evenings.

Enquiry had to be made. Yes of course but

this could have been achieved without the sour air of dishonesty and mistrust.

Why did I choose, as I would later when overhearing that prediction of my future, not to reveal that cross questioning to mother?

Usually placid and certainly not one to present herself at the classroom door at any and every complaint carried home, she had made one exception when Ann, proven to be wrongfully accused of stealing a three-penny piece from her teacher's desk, mother had caught the accuser by the collar flinging her backwards across a table while declaring, 'I don't claim to 'ave raised no angels but I've raised no thief neither! Now I warns you, next time you loses a threepenny bit you be very careful who you accuses o' tekin' it, for next time you won't be let up from that table in one piece!'

Such had been mother's anger, but beneath the anger had been distress, and though there had been no direct accusation made of me, the implications of untoward behaviour were present in an interview mother would have made very plain indeed was not under any circumstances, conducted in the most appropriate manner. It was this further discomfort to mother and not any thought for that of Miss Jones had me keep the whole thing to myself.

Dancing then had been a pleasure from earliest childhood, father's soft shoe shuffle amusing us during those frightening war time evenings, the Black Bottom and Charleston he taught to Hilda and Phoebe. I often think now of how painful it must have been for both of my parents, mother having been born with a badly twisted leg which consequently was encased in a knee length leather boot supported by steel callipers and so could not dance, and father not having the pleasure of whirling her around the dance floor in a quickstep or the ever so daring tango, but they both took pleasure in seeing each of their children delight in that pastime.

Many changes obviously occur once school is left behind, new friends are made and new interests developed but the enjoyment of dancing remained constant and now those occasional visits to the Woden youth club became a weekly Thursday evening recreation.

It was on one such evening asked by a young man would I care to dance, I accepted. Nice manners, easy conversation, a pleasant smile not to mention a competent slow foxtrot had me accept a second invitation to take the floor. Though not Fred Astaire and

Ginger Rogers, our styles seemed to suit and the weeks following saw us become regular partners, both at the Woden and the Saturday evening Darlaston Town Hall dance.

Whether Thursday or Saturday those evenings ended the same, he and his friends bidding myself and the girls I was with goodnight at the door of the hall. There the interest faded, Jack as I had come to know him, never asking as did some other 'bar supports', lads not overkeen on leaving their drinks until the last waltz provided the opportunity for them to ask the question every girl in the hall was familiar with, 'can I see you home?'

I asked no surname nor offered mine, the same with addresses, we danced together, no more was asked or expected. It was a surprise then when one evening sent to empty the teapot onto the garden, mother of the firm belief cold tea was beneficial to certain of her beloved plants, I found Jack and several of his mates grouped at our garden gate. How had he found where I lived? Why were they here? Anxious for them all to leave before mother discovered their presence and demanded to know what I myself could only puzzle over, 'what are they doing here?' I asked them in a tone which could not be mistaken for that of welcome, to 'go away'; but fiery as I have ever been I think in retrospect the request might not have been made in quite such polite terms. Come Thursday evening questions were answered. It had been his intent, had I but given time to ask, would I go with him to the cinema? Had the rest of them accompanied him to give moral support? No. He laughed. Truth was one of them had been told where I lived and when Jack had said he would take a walk along Dangerfield Lane, they had replied friendship insisted they go with him; they had been passing the house, so he claimed, just at the moment I, teapot in hand, appeared in the garden.

Yes, we went to the cinema together gradually the next few months finding us more in each other's company.

Mother, wisely seeing it preferable to know the company kept of each of her daughters, allowed Jack to call at the house and after some while and many refusals on my part, I finally visited his home.

The 'ordeal' was lightened by a very kind Mister and Missis Foster who no doubt understood from the pinkness of my cheeks the shyness I was suffering on meeting them. Their pleasant acceptance of the visitor Jack had sprung upon them was echoed in that of his sisters. Both older than his eighteen years they treated me on that and each subsequent visit as though I too were a sister.

It was around this time my latest craze was knitting. Combining fair isle designs with my 'poor' eye for colour combinations the pullovers and jumpers which came off my needles were, to put it kindly, rather loud. Yellow, bright canary yellow, was the background colour of a trio of matching pullovers I knitted, one for myself, one for Jack ... which with the courage of a Trojan he wore ... and a small one for his young nephew. I presented this to Jack's sister Kathleen and though she must have thought it garish she promptly put it on her little boy, he at least finding the range of colours interesting.

Nancy, Jack's second sister, making preparation for her wedding very kindly issued me with an invitation. By this time more comfortable with the family I was pleased to accept. Sharing the happy occasion as their guest I wished them every happiness. Contact being lost long ago I cannot repeat that wish verbally but I hope the happiness they felt on that special day flavoured every day of their life together.

Given the way Jack was received by my

family and I by his, given those evenings we spent with each other was my dance partner to become my boyfriend? The signs might have been pointing that way but Fate, ever the mistress, had other notions.

Hilda who, as you will recall, had moved to live in the North East was pregnant with her second child. Letters home redolent with an air of longing for parents and sisters, mother decided since Hilda could not leave home to stay with us for the remainder of her pregnancy, then one of the four sisters must go stay with her until after the baby was born.

Phoebe, married with a child, a husband and a home of her own to care for could not be called upon to be away several months.

So then there were three!

Joan of course was still at school and so could not be considered.

Then there were two!

Ann was a most eligible candidate. Ann would go spend time with Hilda. Ann though had already decided otherwise. That germ which forever had her directing the rest of us was alive and well. It would not be practical sending her. A manager down to her toes she had it all worked out. Margaret was earning less than she and accordingly contributed less to the family purse, was it not therefore more sensible Margaret be the sister to go?

Then there was one!

Ann? Providence? Saturday ... five days ahead.

Not a great deal of time, but it wasn't time that mattered; still being fairly limited as far as wardrobe went an hour would see a suitcase packed.

So the problem?

Five sisters reared with one parental edict, 'care for each other, be there for one another through thick and thin' it was no hardship for me to go live with Hilda for any length of time; then, as today, one sister entering the house of the other is seen as being at home.

So again, where was the problem? The problem was my job.

I liked my work. In the few months of being employed at 'Dovaston Marine Engineering' there had, unlike the time employed at 'Appleyards Drapery', not been a single day in which I had wished otherwise. I enjoyed the company, the banter, the friendly atmosphere, now I was to give it all up.

Monday came. I would have to tell the boss I was leaving. Unhappy with the thought of my reason for doing so possibly not being thought entirely truthful I worked the whole day with one eye on the door to the yard watching its every opening for a glimpse of the familiar cream and red shooting brake car which would herald his arrival. The car did not arrive!

At break time next morning sat grouped around the small central iron stove, mugs of tea Margaret the firm's secretary had brewed warming cold fingers, I rehearsed in my mind the words which had played in it the whole of the previous day.

'Mister Dovaston I have to... Mister Dovaston I won't be...'

'What's the matter with you?' It was Norman posed the question and when I shook my head went on, 'You 'ad your eye on that door the whole of yesterday and you are watchin' it again today; it ain't likely to get down from its hinges and walk away.'

No, the door was not about to walk away, but I was.

'Your mother...? I mean her ain't 'ad a fall or anythin' the roads be treacherous wi' all this ice.'

Knowing mother was crippled from birth Doris' question was full of kind concern, she turning her attention to skewering a folded slice of buttered bread onto a knife then holding it to the base of the stove where the glow of the coke fire would toast it while I assured her mother had suffered no accident.

Toward midday, resetting a cutting tool in my machine, Norman caught the glare I sent toward the door.

'Look Marg,' he said using as did everybody else the shortened version of my name, 'if there's anythin' I can do ... what I'm sayin' is there ain't nothin' worth losin' fingers for an' that's what be liable to 'appen with your attention bein' too much on that door.'

I knew what he was saying was for my own good, any machinery when in operation needed total concentration, pay it less and accidents were a promise waiting to be fulfilled.

Perhaps telling Norman what troubled me would help sort the words refusing to come into line, would rationalise the explanation I was finding so difficult to construct.

Perhaps it was his years spent with the Army in the deserts of North Africa sharing problems with mates listening to their worries had developed the patience with which Norman listened to that of a young girl. It must have sounded if not silly, then completely trivial but if he harboured such thought he did not show it.

'Look,' he said wiping his hands on an oil stained rag, 'the gaffer's got teeth but he can't bite your 'ead off. Just go into the office an' tell him the truth; the most he can do is sack you on the spot an' seein' you be leavin' anyway then you ain't lost nothin'.'

That afternoon crossing the yard to fill a bucket of water to mix with machine oil to provide the 'slurry' which must play over cutting tools in order to prevent damage caused by the friction of metal grinding against metal, I saw the cream and red car stood outside the office. I can hear you laughing but it is true when I say half the contents of that bucket spilled over my feet while I stood trying to make up my mind should I knock on that office door or simply drop the bucket and run.

Looking back it seems hardly credible I should have felt as I did, but then so much of our yesterdays were so different to our todays.

I did knock on that door, I did explain the reason of my giving notice and as Norman had predicted my head was not bitten off; but the half smile gathered in the eyes watching as I spoke reawakened my earlier supposition my reason would not be seen as the 'whole truth and nothing but the truth.'

This was confirmed when the sceptical smile in the eyes transferred to the lips the boss saying simply, 'in that case I'll keep your cards 'til you get back.'

No other position could be obtained without producing Employment Cards so if what I had related were a lie then I would be forced to admit to it. Obviously he was testing his theory though at that time it did not register with me.

I know I smiled delighted at the magnanimity of his offer, I remember my exact reply, 'thank you, that is very kind of you.' What I also remember was the so quickly changing smile. He had called my bluff and been proven wrong but appreciation of honesty had become immediately apparent. I would be welcome to return to 'Dovaston Marine Engineering' just as soon as I could.

CHAPTER FIVE

Just as mother had been uninformed of the time of my arrival home following the holiday Mary Green and I had spent with Hilda, so was Hilda similarly uninformed of the day chosen for me to once more return to stay with her. Strange as such behaviour can be thought, and certainly it was not the most practical, with my family it was perfectly normal. We were sisters, we didn't need to say but simply to do, and so I did.

Arriving at Newcastle Central Station at eight o'clock at night alone and having no idea of where was the house Hilda and the family had moved to since that former visit, I admit to feeling more than apprehensive. Where to get the bus? And which bus? To where even if I found the bus depot? There was only one way ... take a taxi! And if the driver should ask direction? Cross that bridge when I come to it!

Hiring a taxi was something I had never done in my life, money did not run to luxuries such as that. Nor could I telephone the house for that too was a luxury as yet in the future. I thought of the money in my pocket, the one pound and several pence given back from my wage packet the evening before and the three pounds mother had added to it, less than five pounds altogether! Would that be sufficient payment for a taxi? Should I ask that question first or should I just get into the car and pray?

Deciding the latter to be the better course

of action, after all if the driver found I hadn't enough cash with which to pay then common sense said he would not take the fare, and also once I reached my sister's home she would help settle any shortfall, so the decision made I picked up my suitcase.

I cannot deny the trembling in my stomach. I ought to have written Hilda informing her of the day and time I would be arriving, if I had she would have been here at the station to meet me and I would not be feeling as scared as I did.

However as mother would have said had she been alongside of me, 'this cock don't fight nor do it lay eggs', meaning standing there doing nothing would not sort the problem. Yet it had to be sorted if I wasn't to sleep that night on a railway platform. Easier thought than done! Suitcase in hand I walked out into the night.

'Ye lewk over dowie hinny.'

A man stood at the roadside ... was he speaking to me? Uncertain and not a little perturbed I glanced along the street. Was this where I might find a taxi or was there some depot same as for buses?

'Where ye after gannin'?'

The man *was* speaking to me, his direct look said so, but what was it he had said?

What language had he spoken? Not that it would have made any difference for the only language in which I could converse or understand was English and he definitely was not speaking in that.

A policeman! Why hadn't I thought of that before, a policeman would be sure to direct me; the only problem with that was where to find a policeman? I had not noticed one in the railway station and I certainly could not see one in the street.

'Haway...'

'Haway!' That one expression ringing in my ears I didn't hear the rest of what the man was now saying; as though to a lifebelt I clung to that one word, a word I had heard Hilda' s husband use many times. Maybe, if I spoke slowly, if I tried extra carefully to pronounce my words clearly he just might understand I wanted to find a taxi.

Put to the test the theory was met with a laugh.

'Ye mevvies misdooted,' he smiled, 'when I said where ye gannin' I was askin' did you want a taxi? But divven fach y'sel, we aal gets to misunderstand. Now, where be it y'be stoppin'?'

Still a little scared it took some moments for my brain to interpret his reply and to recognise the latter part was enquiry as to where it was I wished to be taken. Thank Heaven I did at least know my sister's address.

'Seventeen Northumberland Place, Chester-le-Street,' he repeated handing my suitcase into the car, 'why aye pet, I knaas where that be.'

Relieved the hurdle of how to reach my destination was cleared and trying not to return to that of maybe having insufficient funds to pay for my taxi ride I attempted to join in conversation but with most of what was said lost on me, my replies of 'yes' or 'no' must have been totally inane; the poor driver probably wondering had he picked up a stray from a mental institution.

But stressful as that last half hour had been it did not completely undermine the thrill of adventure provided by my having travelled alone, neither did it reduce the pleasure I had revelled in the whole of those long hours sat in that train, the joy of surprise I was about to spring on my sister, of seeing her delight at our being together. So it was. My three pounds proving more than enough to pay the taxi fare I decided to add a little more flavour to the dish. Instead of walking straight into the house I knocked on the door.

Waiting in the almost pitch darkness of the small porch set at the rear door I hugged delight to myself. This was going to be such a surprise.

And was it? Oh yes. But not for Hilda. It was not she came to answer that knock. The door opening showed, outlined by light from the kitchen, the man who twice had asked a very young Margaret would she marry him.

Of course I had known he lived in that house but had paid no attention to the fact, why would I? It would have no effect on me ... or so I thought. Standing speechless staring at the figure in the shadows it was evident my sudden arrival had a marked effect on him.

'Well!' I asked after several moments of silence, 'are you going to ask me in?'

My question was answered by Hilda who having heard me speak called out, but standing aside for me to enter her brother-in-law said not a word.

Ralph, the young man who had spent his weekend leaves at my parents' home, who had given so much of that time to me had not uttered a word on opening the door to that unexpected visitor, nor did he speak at all the remainder of the evening. Had I done something to annoy him? Had he taken refusals of his proposals of marriage as a cold snub, was it that rankling now? No, he was too sensible for that! So had he over time realised the absurdity of proposing to so young a girl that now it was embarrassing to him?

Caught up in the flurry of arrival, of answering numerous questions as to the well-being of everyone at home, of relating over and again the doings of each sister; Phoebe's latest entrepreneurial schemes and their inevitable failure, Ann's frequent turnover of boyfriends, Joan's progress at school and of course my own activities I nevertheless felt a little hurt at this lack of interest on Ralph's part, even more so when as describing Jack Foster and the evenings we danced together Ralph gave me one withering look and promptly walked out.

Thinking of this later I attempted to analyse the reason for his lack of welcome, of his unusual silence. Could it be that now demobbed and at home, and once more with the company of his friends he no longer held any interest or desire to rekindle a friendship he had formed while on National Service? Was his ignoring of me a way of relating this?

That analysis however seemed disproved

when the following weekend I was invited to accompany him and a group of his friends on their usual Sunday afternoon jaunt to the town's large park. But though walking beside me he remained silent leaving it to those others to make conversation with a girl whose accent they obviously found difficult to understand, while to my ears their every other word might well have been any language but English. But possibly due to trailing me along everywhere they went becoming too much of a drag the group eventually broke up leaving just one, Ralph's childhood and virtually inseparable friend John Pickard. Sixty years on they are still the best of mates.

One Sunday afternoon preceding the dissolution of the self styled 'Birtley Boys' the group decided on a walk along the Wear, the river which runs through Chester-le-Street on its travels to the North Sea.

More on sufferance I think than on pleasure of her company an invitation was extended to Ralph's protégé. Sandwiched as always between Ralph and John Pickard the banter of the others walking a little ahead did not sit easy with me, somehow I felt slightly apprehensive. Why? They had treated me no differently to other occasions of being in their company. Intuition proved sound when it was suggested we all take a boat on the river. It needed no detailed explanation. I knew instinctively the intention was with me as a passenger to get the boat onto open water then set it rocking. Young I may have been but stupid I definitely was not. If they wanted to play Superman they would have no Lois Lane in the shape of Margaret Astbury to 'rescue', she was not prepared to assist any display of macho tendencies. A pleasant smile hiding the thought I declined the invitation resisting all cajoling with a firm 'I prefer to walk.' Intuition had prepared me for one thing but not for Ralph climbing into that boat. I couldn't believe he would leave me alone in a place I had no knowledge of! His way of saying if I wanted to be with him then I would get into that boat? It might very well have been that way but then such reasoning was clouded by one overriding thought ... he preferred being with his mates rather than with me! Crestfallen but determined not to allow what felt like the sharp stab of a knife to be seen by the watching group I waved as the rest of the lads clambered aboard. Is sixth sense a gift shared by male and female? Had John Pickard in some way defined that sudden sting or seen the shadow of it flash across my face? Sympathy? Natural good manners? Or the kindness I would come to know so well? At that moment I could not have said, I only felt grateful when he too declined that boat trip electing instead to remain with me. I had known several partings during the time since Ralph and I first met, weekend passes, embarkation leave and of course after that last visit following demobilisation. All of these had ended with goodbyes and each had left me with a vague sense of emptiness, that 'something is missing' sort of feeling which was always a little more rueful than might have been expected from a parting with a casual acquaintance, yet quite why that should be so I never understood, nor yet could I define the look on Ralph's face as that boat pulled away or the sensation I felt deep inside myself, a pain so cutting as to be almost physical.

Too hurt to broach the subject or not wanting to hear in so many words that my company was not quite so welcome as it had been those times he had been a visitor to Dangerfield Lane? Whichever, no reference was made to the incident by either of us that evening nor on any of the following occasions I was invited along on walks, though

John Pickard sensing the tension between Ralph and myself made every effort to include me in the conversation.

There were relatively few times in all of the weeks spent at his home that Ralph and I were left solely in each other's company; weekday evenings being spent with Hilda and the family; but she mindful as she had ever been of a younger sister realised work without play was not the most favourable of situations and so on Saturdays made no objection to my going with her brother-in-law and his friend John Pickard to the 'Apollo' the local cinema, or to the Sunday dance sometimes held at what the locals called the 'Welfare', a clubhouse similar to the 'Woden' at Darlaston. This was a strange experience for me, I was more familiar with dances which began at eight p.m. not at midnight which due to Sunday licensing laws this one did. Time there was short lived, work commitment next day requiring both John and Ralph to leave long before the dance ended. Why we went at all is still a mystery; neither of the two could dance and with them stood one at each shoulder like personal bodyguards no other potential partner however well meaning or even sympathetic proved compassionate enough to attempt to pluck a wallflower from between two prickles. A dance without dancing! I ask again, why on earth did we go?

Was it being always in the company of others precluded my making mention of the afternoon of the boat trip or was it more truly the fact of telling Ralph he had no need to feel any obligation to spend time with me? Though in all honesty thinking how to say this once opportunity arrived was painful in itself. Opportunity though, like the proverbial bad penny, did eventually turn up.

Mom and Dad had come to spend Christmas with Hilda and prior to returning home to Wednesbury mother decided on shopping in Newcastle. She, Hilda and myself ready to leave were joined by Ralph who also wished to shop in the city and so travelled there with us. The afternoon spent in various shops, mother more than ready for her 'nice cup o' tea', we walked to the bus station meeting again with Ralph who sprang the surprise of two seats booked for the pantomime showing at the 'Empire' theatre and with mother's nod of permission and no time given me to think much less refuse, swept me from the bus queue. As had once happened so long before he held my hand throughout the performance except this time for me it did not feel like a brotherly gesture but brought a rapid beat to the pulses, a catch in the throat, a tightness in the chest, all in all a totally bewildering experience, which did not end when, the show over, we left the theatre. My hand caught firmly in his, the silence of that wordless bus ride home was obliterated by a pounding in my ears. I wanted that touch yet I knew it was not meant to bring such emotion, that it was a touch of friendship and I must read no more into it than that. This then was the moment he had to be told there was no compulsion on his part to give time to me. How to say it? How to get the words past the lump in my throat? Questions repeated in my mind with every step yet each asking bringing the same reply. You have to say it and it has to be now!

A few more yards along the darkened street we would have reached the house and there with all the family present the chances of saying anything of what was in my mind would be gone. Pulling my hand free, I began what I intended as a reprieve from what for Ralph could be no more than a duty, repayment in kind of the concord afforded him during those leaves from the Army.

'You thought that?' he said as my explanation fumbled to a halt, 'it couldn't be further from the truth. Why do you think it was you and no one else I chose to be with on those leaves? Why do you think I stay in the house in the evenings instead of going out with the lads? It is because *you* are there, because I want to be with *you* as long as I can.'

'So why leave me behind and go off on a boat!'

A retort on my part rather than a query his answer was a quick disparaging laugh. 'That was to answer a question of my own. I had to find out can I part from you? Lord knows it was hard enough all those times before... I don't think I can face that again.'

Catching my hand he went on softly, 'I love you, I've loved you from first seeing you on that railway platform and if you look inside yourself you'll see you've known as much all along. I realise the mess I made of asking you to marry me, it was stupid threatening you the way I did but I was so scared of losing you. What I should have said was will you marry me when you are old enough? And I'm asking the same now, I won't care how long I wait if only you will say yes.'

Caught close to him in that dark lane listening to his whispered, 'I love you, you'll never know how much I love you', I knew then he could have all my life in which to tell me.

CHAPTER SIX

Used to helping clean mother's house at weekends, housework at number Seventeen was no major shock though in the later days of her pregnancy Hilda reluctantly admitting to tiredness, I found coping with washing and ironing for Hilda's husband, father-in-law and brother-in-law, her young son plus the two of us something of an eye opener. How, crippled in arm and leg, had my mother managed cooking, cleaning and laundry for five daughters and a husband with no more than a broom, a scrubbing brush and a dolly tub? There were no niceties of vacuum cleaner or washing machine, the arrival of an electric iron happening only after her girls were grown up.

But every day found Hilda and I laughing, or sometimes in my case blushing. One garment never seen in number fifty one Dangerfield Lane was 'Long Johns', waist to ankle underpants worn by some men. My first encounter with what appeared to me to be a somewhat bizarre article was one such 'wash day.' Bringing clothes indoors from the line strung across the garden, folding them preparatory to ironing there came the turn of the 'Long Johns'. Resistance was useless. Pinning a shirt to the pants I held the 'figure' close. Tango, rumba, old fashioned waltz, my 'partner' and I sashayed around the room, both Hilda and myself giggling like ten year olds ... giggling that was until halfway through a swoop worthy of the finest Argentinian Tango master I saw, watching from the doorway, the owner of my 'Latin lover.' Whatever her father-in-law made of my bid for world champion ballroom dancer he never shared the opinion with me.

Paul, my four year old nephew liked helping auntie, making numerous imaginary journeys to the shops 'purchasing' many, and thankfully just as imaginary items. One favourite always included a 'tin of salmon with currants in.' Uggh! Another uggh! was a 'sausage with custard.' Paul, needless to say did not become a chef.

Each of us sisters bore very close resemblance, barely a difference in looks, height and colouring. Not surprising then when my having taken to wearing Hilda's maternity smocks while working in the house Paul would often mistake one for the other, his looks at me when told, 'I'm not your mom' clearly saying why did we not sort ourselves out! Paul though was not alone in his misconception. The same mistake happened one evening. Washing dishes at the kitchen sink, dressed in the usual garb of maternity smock I couldn't but smile when Bill, Hilda's husband, came in from work and coming up behind me put his arms around my waist. Restraining a giggle I said softly, 'I'll tell our Hilda.' Poor Bill, he jumped away quicker than a rocket on Guy Fawkes' night. Hilda and I thought it hilarious but ever after that Bill took care in determining which sister was which.

February seventh, Hilda's second child, a boy, was born and a month later I was returning home to Wednesbury minus the engagement ring Ralph had bought for me and which after a fit of pique on my part during which I had thrown it at him he had flicked it into the fire saying, 'if you don't want it it's no good to me.' Didn't want it! I had minutely searched the ashes next morning when cleaning the fireplace but my precious ring was gone. He wanted to replace it that next day but I wouldn't hear of that, after all we didn't need a ring did we?

Setting away for Newcastle Central Station much earlier than required simply in order to have that extra time alone we were both very subdued. It was the moment we both knew had to come but now it had actually arrived to say we felt miserable is a positive understatement. Purchasing my ticket we were advised of the train due to leave in five minutes and of a further one which would leave for Birmingham at five thirty. Four and a half hours more we could be together. It needed no discussion ... the one o'clock train left without me!

North East weather in March is more often than not unsuitable for simply strolling and that Saturday was no exception with a fiercely cold wind biting past coats and gloves. But how to get out of it? Where to go for those hours? The parks were too cold and the shops held no interest. The solution came in the shape of a cinema. We of course would not be alone but the warm semi darkness would in some measure provide the privacy we both wanted. I don't recall either of us checking the title of the film nor did it truly matter when I found myself watching 'Red Hot and Blue' starring Betty Hutton, never anywhere near a favourite actress of mine. We had tried to stave off the unhappy event but as with all things time came to finally board that train. It was the most heart tearing moment I had ever experienced when, his face drawn with emotion, Ralph closed the compartment door his lips forming those words he had whispered in the lane the evening I had agreed one day we would marry; 'you'll never know how much I love you.' I knew my feelings for him, tears falling for most of that journey to Birmingham attesting to my own pain of separation.

Wrapped up in each other Ralph and I had paid no mind to the fact of my being met at Birmingham, neither in the cloud of unhappiness fogging my mind at our parting did it register with me. The fog however was soon blown away when alighting from the carriage a shout of 'where on earth have you been? We've waited all day for you!' A none too pleased Ann frowned, then all forgiving hugged me dismissing the reason of my having misread the train times as 'easily done.' I never did reveal the truth, Ann never has learned the real reason of my non arrival on that earlier train, but being the sisters we have always been, I know there will be a laugh and another hug should she ever come to read of my 'fib.'

Returned to my family, resuming my job at Dovaston's life was not in those following two weeks quite the pleasant routine it had been prior to my going away. Everything followed its regular path, mother and dad loving as ever, my sisters readily sharing of their day's experiences, even Jack Foster called regularly offering an evening at the cinema or one of the local dance halls. I recognised the kindness behind the invitations but nevertheless refused, suddenly I had no desire to socialise. I had slipped easily into my job at the factory, at home I laughed – and argued – with my sisters; on the surface everything appeared as normal yet for me the world felt strangely vacant, the heart of it was missing.

Mother, who never missed anything affecting either of her daughters, saw quite clearly the feelings I was trying to hide. For the first two weeks following my return she said nothing, regarding with silence my most unusual refusing to go dancing, my staying home each evening after work. Wisely, I now realise, she was giving me time, time to come to terms with myself, to determine what it was I truly wanted. There, in the middle of the third week, father gone for his favourite game of cards at the pub, Ann out with the latest in a string of boyfriends and Joan at the cinema with her friends, mom and I alone in the house she said, 'what happened to the ring?'

Blushing deep pink I struggled with a conscience which should have pricked when I accepted that engagement ring but it hadn't; now it pricked the harder. We should have written to my parents, asked their permission to take the step we had ... now I must face the music.

'We ... we should have asked...'

'Wouldn't 'ave med any difference.' She said smiling at my embarrassment, 'might 'ave delayed things for a while but it wouldn't no way have put him off altogether; the lad loves you, he loves the very ground you walk on, that was obvious right from the start. I seen it plain and so did his brother, oh yes...' she nodded as a fresh tide of colour deepened in my cheeks, 'I talked with Bill following the first couple of times Ralph came to this house and he in turn must have discussed what we could all see happening for the answer to my questions was "Ralph feels for Margaret what I feel for Hilda." Now that be all well and good but for me and your dad the most important question is how do you feel about the lad?'

She was asking did I love him? If I told her would she dismiss it as a girlish infatuation, tell me I was far too young to harbour such emotions? The thought flashed but was as quickly replaced by another. Mother never dismissed out of hand anything her girls brought to her; she always listened, comforted and advised, why would she behave otherwise now?

'I thought...'

I paused swallowing hard, searching for words that seemed so hard to find.

'I thought once ... once I was home it would be alright, that the hurt I felt on the train would disappear and I wouldn't miss him so much but...'

'But it ain't gone away.' She shook her head as my admission tailed off. 'No need to tell me, I can see in your eyes you miss him and it don't need the asking does he miss you, all that does need deciding is what to do about it. Letters be one thing, they keep you in touch but they don't take the place of them that writes 'em; getting to know, to *really* know whether what you feel now will still be your feelings in a year or so won't come from reading nor writing of letters, that will come only from each other's company.'

'Ralph feels the same way,' I answered, 'he says in his letter he intends to do as Bill did, come to look for work and lodgings either in Wednesbury or Darlaston, that way we can see each other more often.'

'Your dad and me thought that to be what would 'appen and we both be of the same mind...'

She was going to advise against it! Tell me it would make more sense for him to remain at home, give himself a while longer before taking such a step! Disappointment lodging firmly in my throat I almost cried relief when she went on.

'...tell the lad if he be inclined to live with us then he can have the middle bedroom; won't be the first time you three wenches have shared a room, and as for a job your dad says he can get him one along of Newman's Tubes.'

A week later Ralph was living at fifty one Dangerfield Lane, mother finding in him the son she had always longed for and he responding with a deep affection which never faltered and far from feeling resentment at once more having to sleep three to a room, Ann and Joan accepted him as readily as they had on each occasion of those Army leaves, in fact he was immediately a 'brother' to each of four sisters.

This then was the beginning of mother's 'proving' period. As with many other young people paths were not always bathed in sunshine, there were stormy moments; 'Mardy Marg' the epithet my sisters had given a toddler who sulked in order to get her own way, still merited use on occasions, several of these resulting in my telling Ralph to leave, that I no longer wanted him: thank heavens for his patience.

June Nineteen Fifty. The year of my parents' silver wedding anniversary and this time an 'official' engagement for Ralph and myself. The effects of the war were still being very much felt, restrictions applied to pretty much everything, the few they didn't proving more than a little expensive, but as ever mother was determined to mark the event as best she could. Exchanging a pound of sugar for a packet of butter, a quarter of tea for a bag of flour, the system of exchange and mart which so often prevailed among neighbours attempting to bring a festive air to some celebration eventually proving sufficient, mother worked that particular magic which produced 'spreads' for wartime weddings and V.E. parties until it seemed her own table could hold no more.

'Now don't you lot go spendin' your money on presents, your dad and me 'ave all we wants and you don't 'ave money to go wastin' on things as ain't needed!'

Mother's instruction that no gifts were needed to mark her special day had been ignored. With each presentation and the murmured 'I love you mom, I love you dad', a few more tears fell but behind them was the smile, that special smile which spoke loudly of pride in their family.

Hugs and kisses finally over, mother turned to where Ralph and I sat. 'It don't only be our day', she smiled, 'it be your day as well so come on lad, bring out that ring I know you've got in your pocket.'

We had not told anyone of our going to purchase a second engagement ring but as with so many things mother needed no telling. Truth was I had not wished for one but Ralph had insisted saying my wearing his ring made him feel, in those now old fashioned words, 'I was truly his'. But I had already wasted his money when throwing the first ring into the fire! The guilt of this weighed heavily that Saturday morning we went to West Bromwich and the weight did not lift while viewing rings in Baker's Jewellery shop, consequently I chose the smallest stone on display. Tiny those diamonds are but for me they outshine the Koh-I-Noor!

CHAPTER SEVEN

The combined celebration of my parents' silver wedding and a daughter's engagement was quickly followed by yet one more. September saw the introduction of Ann's latest boyfriend. Tall, bronzed from National Service in Hong Kong, Ray Dibble was afforded the same cordiality our parents showed to the friends of each of their girls invited to the house. Ann, proud of her handsome new conquest spent most of her evenings with him. She had found her Mister Right and in November she became Missis Raymond Dibble. But surprise as this might have been for mother and father there was another close at hand.

'You will marry me, even if you have to!'

Spoken so many months before those words returned to haunt. Saying nothing to anyone I waited for Nature's sign my sin would not find me out. But Nature's sign did not come. How...? Why...? Questions which must have so many times been asked by women ran incessantly in my mind.

'...*even if you have to!*'

Had what had been done a deliberate move on Ralph's part? No! I refused the thought trying to dominate all others, a thought I knew even in my distress was offering me a way to escape all blame, all responsibility. He wanted to be married but he would not have it purposely this way. There had been kisses yes, but until that one time nothing more. That one time! I have read that when something you have done, something you are responsible for comes real and very profound heartache, the mind buries it so deep in the psyche it cannot be remembered. Maybe that is the reason all memory of that 'fall from grace' has never returned. Many incidents flick into the mind in moments of relaxation; recollections happy and sad, of laughter and joy, sometimes of anxiety or fear, but though having experienced a fair share of each emotion during my life, not once has the briefest glimpse of that moment of weakness surfaced, no memory crept back from those subconscious depths; but though the act may have been resigned to oblivion the shame for what I had done would remain for many years.

How to tell my parents I was pregnant? How to say we had betrayed the trust they had placed in Ralph and myself?

'It's my fault'. Holding me close Ralph tried to still the tears I couldn't hold back. 'It's down to me to tell them, they will understand the only excuse I have to offer is that I love you, a love I've had from the instant of setting eyes on a bad tempered thirteen year old, I think your mom and dad know this, that they know that love will never alter. It isn't the way I would have chosen, God knows I would die before I hurt you but this...' his arms tightening, his lips touching my face he went on softly, '...this has given me the one thing I want more than anything in the world, you as my wife.'

But with five or so months yet before reaching the age of eighteen and therefore being of legal age to marry, parental consent would be needed. Would I be given that permission or would my parents deem me too young to embark on such a commitment?

Wartime had relaxed many rules of social behaviour but the obloquy attached to unwed mothers was in Nineteen Fifty One still very much prevalent while the modern practice of partners living together outside of marriage or ... heaven forbid ... a child born a bastard ... carried an even more painful stigma.

Are events, any event of history truly a one off? Does Fate satisfy itself with a single bite of human frailty or having savoured the sweetness of bitter fruits does it slip away, hiding in the shadows of the past, waiting there for the opportunity to eat once more from the dish of mortification and regret? Certainly it had remained at my mother's shoulder, biding time, waiting to feast again on desirable morsels of guilt and remorse, to taste afresh the flavour of conscience and self reproach it had relished with her own fall from grace. But where Fate had been successful twenty six years before it was now to fail.

Knowing the depth of Ralph's feelings for me, realising in all probability the chance of history repeating itself, perhaps it could be thought a mistake on my parents' part in allowing him to share their home. But mother had experienced for herself the strength of emotion love can create, she had lived the moment the results of those emotions must be faced and if, like herself, her daughter's world crashed then it would crash where she was there to pick up the pieces.

Disappointment, as surely in their hearts my parents must have felt, none showed in their receiving of Ralph's confession. No vilification, no condemnation, only the love and understanding they had shown all of my life. Nor for my sisters was blame to enter into the proceedings.

The hostilities of war, the accompanying dreads and fears encountered during those awful years might be ended but the strictures of them were still being felt with food rationing and the virtual impossibility of obtaining goods once so complacently taken for granted. But no matter the shortages and no matter with the help of heaven or hell the family were determined this wedding would be the very best they could provide. Not for 'our Marg' the brief Registry Office ceremony both Hilda and Ann had chosen; not for her the borrowed bridal gown and attendants' dresses lent for Phoebe's wedding on the proviso the lender's relative be one of the bridesmaids, for this sister they were determined the 'something old ... something borrowed' would be unacceptable, all would be new and hers alone.

With this view in mind the three weeks

needed for calling the Banns were spent in a flurry of where to find this? How do we get that? And what about those? The discussions pleasurable to mom, Phoebe, Ann and Joan held none of that emotion for me. I felt only misery at what I had done, I couldn't muster so much as a smile, but even so mother would have no reprimand given, no saying by the rest of her family to 'pull yourself together, what's done is done and you just have to get on with it!' even though they might secretly have wished she would.

Saturday following the first calling of the Banns in the church of All Saints at Moxley, Ann, now living at the home of her husband's parents, came to visit with mother. While shopping in Walsall she had watched a plain gold ring being set in pride of place in the window of a small jewellery shop in the centre of town.

'You should go see it our Marg...'
She tried to instil enthusiasm into me.

'...Looking at it I'd say it's likely twenty two carat; one thing I am sure of is it won't be in that window for long, somebody will snatch it up.'

Who cares! Guilt and misery had the thought cry in my mind. I didn't want to look at any ring. Why couldn't my family chastise me, why couldn't they reproach, condemn the wrong I had done!

Caught in my own unhappiness I could not see, as my mother and father did, that far from easing the sting of conscience condemnation would only add to suffering. She had felt the blows of an angry father, cried under the lash of his tongue while her husband had lived a lifetime of silent reproof and resentment from the man who never forgave the shame brought on his name; they had not forgotten that which was after all the consequence of a moment of failure, the bitterness which had been the result.

I have often thought over the years that my mother had been endowed with some sort of extra sensory perception. Certainly she seemed that morning to tune into my thoughts. Quietly, with no smile she said, 'I knows what you be goin' through, I knows the regret, but I also knows you 'ave a lad who worships you. Like me and your dad you might have a lifetime of hard work, you might never 'ave more than two pennies to rub together but with that lad you'll 'ave a wealth of love; now go buy that ring.'

I smile now remembering Ann's exuberance over something which to modern eyes is of little significance. But more than half a century ago, probably because imports of food and other crucial necessities so outweighed the importance of gold there was a fear of the metal joining the long list of 'unobtainable'. Certainly wedding rings became ever more narrow, some though of government 'utility' standard resembling nothing more than a strand of wire and these mainly nine carat. That then explains the elderly jeweller's words as he handed to me his prized exhibit.

'That's one of the old ones'. An elderly man, the jeweller looked lovingly at the gleaming gold band. 'That has been in my safe from soon after the start of the war. There was no knowing would the same be made again so I kept it along of my son being wed.'

'Then you must not sell it!'

A shake of the head accompanying the gentle thrusting of the ring back into my hand, the man swallowed hard before answering. 'My lad won't be the man to slip that on the finger of his bride, he was killed at Dunkirk.'

What was my sadness compared to that man's? Yet he could smile. The ring in Ralph's pocket, my hand firmly in his, I tried to reason, but it would be a long time before I could truly come to terms with myself.

Friday the second of February Nineteen Fifty One. The day before my wedding. I was sitting dejectedly in the living room when father asked, 'Wheer y' goin' to live cock, after y'be married?'

Another bombshell!

Ralph and I had lived in cloud cuckoo land since his taking up residence in Dangerfield Lane, a land where nothing controversial seemed to gain admittance. But suddenly there was a question which either born of naivety or downright thoughtless stupidity didn't matter, all that did matter was I had no answer.

A few moments of silence telling father all there was to be told I felt the gentle pressure of his hand on my shoulder, heard the quiet beloved voice say softly 'you'll live 'ere wi' we.'

Saturday, and to use a popular phrase, the moment of truth had arrived. Mother, Hilda, Ann and her husband Ray had left to walk to church. No money for bridal cars. However a middle aged couple with whom Phoebe had struck up friendship since her house move to Kings Hill had offered to drive the bride and attendants the short distance to Moxley. Sister Joan then in mauve taffeta bridesmaid dress and young nephews Paul and Andrew in traditional page boy dress complete with black patent silver buckle shoes were whisked away.

Father, Phoebe and me.

Stood waiting for the return of the loaned car, it seemed neither of us had a word to say, then with the short hoot of the car horn we moved to the tiny box like hall. 'You don't have to go!' Phoebe had thrown her arms across the door, 'you don't have to go if you don't want to!'

No church organ struck up to announce 'here comes the bride' as dressed in classic style cream silk crepe-de-chine gown complete with full length veil held in place by tiara made of the same material, and holding a small white prayer book, I walked down the aisle on father's arm. Where was the 'floating' I had so often read about? Where the cloud of happiness always supposed to envelop the bride? Lack of wedding cars, bridal bouquets, organ music and church bells could all be understood, no finances available for such niceties, but the feeling lacking inside of me, the joy of at last coming to be joined with the man I loved ...

was it that was my real mistake, was I not after all in love? The answer came when standing in his place beside his best man Ralph turned to watch my approach and the look on his face, the sheer love in his eyes banished every lingering doubt.

I had always thought it the privilege of the bride to be late for her wedding but as the whispers of the guests grew louder I could see there was just one more thing this occasion lacked... A priest!

So where was the man promised to hear our vows? The answer, when John Pickard and a male guest ran the few yards to the vicarage, turned out to be he had forgotten all about the pre-arranged marriage service and was happily digging his garden.

Minutes later, his shoes covered with soil, his cassock stained with dried dribbled food, the priest made his appearance and I at last became Missis Ralph Hutchinson.

One photograph of bride and groom, one photograph of the group of assembled guests, no fabulous album ... just one more financially forbidden item. Returned to my parents' house, waiting for the family to walk back from the church Ralph took from his pocket a piece of broken jewellery. Pressing the small metal heart into my hand he said, 'Didn't I tell you one day these two (heart and key) would be joined together.'

He had kept that half of a broken brooch since taking it from me years before. I looked at our wedding presents, one table cloth and one very small dish and a toaster, but in my hand I had a gift no money could buy.

Looking back on the marriages of my own two daughters, and the yet more recent ever more lavish embellishments deemed so very necessary by the couples of today, I smile and ask myself, truly would all of that add one iota to the love and happiness that has been mine for so many years.

In 'Penny Dip', an autobiography of my Black Country childhood and pre-curser to this later work, I talked of my four sisters, of the way our parents brought us up and their one rule 'stick by one another.' This we did though sometimes it meant a fight with other kids in the Lane. However like most folk we are not without our individual idio-syncrasies. Ann's as we have seen being of managerial tendency, but Phoebe, hers was a very different trait.

From the earliest childhood anything in the house which attracted Phoebe's attention became automatically hers regardless of its true owner. There would be a bit of a to and fro regarding any said item, Phoebe's reply on relinquishing it an airy, 'well I thought you didn't want it!' That would be the end of the matter and quickly forgotten. But there are some, little disputes at the time, have the feelings harsh words elicit not so easily dismissed.

The evening following my wedding Phoebe was visiting Dangerfield Lane. Mother had gone with Hilda to pay a visit to mother's sister which had Phoebe and myself alone in the house. Within moments of her arrival her eye landed on the small package sat on the living room table. 'That's mine!' At the same time her age old words were uttered her hand moved as quickly.

'They are not yours.'

'They am!' Phoebe clutched the cellophane wrapped packet. 'I left 'em here last night!'

'No!' I countered determined to stick to my guns. 'They are mine, they were a good will gift given by the shopkeeper who sold me my wedding dress.'

'Oh.' Phoebe paused and then in her usual airy fashion replied, 'Well you won't be wantin' 'em.'

Why?... Why would I not be wanting them?

I was pregnant, I felt dowdy yes, but surely I was not beyond the pleasure of wearing a pair of ultra fine – oh so difficult to obtain – nylon stockings.

'No!' I said, all of those emotions welling together, 'those are my nylons and you are not having them!'

Had it been one of those monotonously regular rows with her husband, he being the most irrational and difficult man to live with had Phoebe that evening not so gracious in defeat? Whatever the cause a scowl on her face she snatched her hand from the packet saying derisively, 'You're only a lodger 'ere.'

In an instant it seemed my whole world turned upside down. Was that all I was? Had I changed from being a daughter to a paying lodger?

Never once in the eight years Ralph, myself and eventually our daughters shared my parents' home did they ever give me cause to think so; yet even now Phoebe's words sometimes return and each memory brings its shadow of hurt.

CHAPTER EIGHT

Ann married and living with her in-laws in Lowe Avenue, Darlaston; Joan, with our parents' consent, having after my wedding returned to the North East with Hilda to finish her compulsory education there. Hilda still feeling lonely for the family, mother felt one sister might help relieve those feelings – left just Ralph and myself to see Phoebe and her two children safely home after visiting mother.

The fact of my being eight months pregnant made no impression at all on her husband, he following his usual practice of going straight home from the pub. We knew this one particular night had proved no different when father returned alone.

'He's gone 'ome mah wench,' Father told a not surprised Phoebe.

There was nothing for it. She could not be allowed to go home alone. Ralph and I reached for our coats.

It had rained heavily for several hours but now mercifully it had stopped. Olwen, nine months old was snugly wrapped in the bed of the pram, Andrew three years old was sat on the foot of it so we could walk more quickly.

We could go by way of Darlaston crossing the Bull Stake and proceeding along the Wednesbury Road until we reached King's Hill. The drawback with that was distance, it would prove well over half an hour's walk. The alternative was that of going by way of what long years back had been cornfields but now was waste ground covered with slag (the rubbish scooped from molten steel) the jagged heaps of this sharp as razors. But unpleasant as this could be, it reduced the time of getting Phoebe home to a quick ten minutes.

This then was the way we would go.

Phoebe wheeling the pram, her faster step having her a yard or so in front of me, everything was normal – normal until she screamed. Pushing the pram with the children in it in one direction, she racing off in another. Ralph immediately ran for the pram then handing it to me went to get Phoebe.

What had caused the screaming?

The evening rain heavy and prolonged had flushed out scores of tiny yellow frogs, these were hopping across the road glinting like so many golden fairy lights in the radiance of the moon, one of which Phoebe declared had jumped up her leg.

Getting her quietened at last and safely into the house Ralph checked the bedroom to make certain her husband was there, which of course he was, fast asleep and snoring so we began our own return journey.

I thought the episode of the frog had not affected me but no sooner did we set foot on that waste ground than like my sister I began to scream. To this day I don't know why, I only know Ralph tried to calm me saying over and over again, 'stop screaming, folk will think I'm raping you.'

No, Andrew Williams senior never did alter his ways.

Mother and father then had placed no blame on Ralph or myself, in fact they had done their level best to give me a wedding I could not otherwise have hoped for as well as sharing their home with us.

But I knew I had done wrong and if they would not punish us then I must do it myself. To this end I allowed my 'mardy' temper to become even more pronounced.

We didn't deserve to be happy.

That underlying thought lived in my mind for many, many years in itself giving rise to bad temper. I would build the tiniest mole-hills into a mountain.

Take for example the case of the haircut.

It was Friday teatime. Ralph was half an hour late getting home from Rubery Owen engineering works at Darlaston. Not to worry it was his weekly visit to the barber. Sure enough after several minutes he breezed into the kitchen.

What on earth had happened?

Aghast I stared at him; stared at hair cut so high above the ears it almost touched the crown, stared at the back of the head almost totally devoid of hair.

What the hell had he done! Anger rose swiftly.

All he needed was an arrow painted on his jacket to make the perfect picture of a convict!

'Why?' I managed at last.

His answer that having his hair cut short would mean only one visit a month instead of once a week, therefore saving four shillings and eight pence, cut no ice with me. Yes we were desperately short of money, yes he had given up cigarettes for that self same reason, but that haircut... Oh Lord it was atrocious!

All night my emotions simmered until in

bed it all came to a head.

Mother had by this time given us the much larger front bedroom saying we would need the extra space for a cot.

Outside the rain was pelting down, great drops hurling themselves against the window.

Lying in bed I watched Ralph prepare for bed. Shirt and vest removed he went to the bathroom. Now was my chance. Snatching up the pyjamas laid ready to put on I opened the window and threw them out then closed the window and climbed back into bed.

'Where are my pyjamas?' Ralph looked at the spot where they had lain on the bed.

'Outside!' I snapped. 'I've chucked them out the window!'

Now instead of getting another pair as I think I expected he opened the window seeing below on the roof of the living room a sodden yellow pool. In a moment he had climbed down onto the bay and in that same moment Margaret closed the window shutting him out in the pouring rain.

Had I expected to feel some sort of jubilation? Was that childish action supposed to make me feel good? In effect it did neither, it just gave me a sense of foreboding.

He wouldn't stay there in the rain, he

would shin down the drainpipe go around to the back door and hammer on it until father went downstairs to let him in ... that way it would all come to mother's ears!

Now mother was gentle, she was lenient ... but she wasn't daft and neither would she allow her daughters to be, but what I had done was plain daft and tomorrow I would be in for a right tongue lashing.

All this passing swift as a lightning streak through my mind, I flung open the window.

Having climbed inside Ralph took his soaking wet pyjamas to the bathroom, draping them over the bath, then having dried himself returned to the bedroom, dressed in a fresh pair of pyjamas, snapped off the light, climbed into bed and taking me in his arms went straight off to sleep.

Patience? My husband could teach the Biblical Job a thing or two about patience.

That was the first of the short back and sighs but as the future would reveal it was not to be the last.

Mother's care during the horrid months of morning sickness which with me lasted all day and every day must have added enormously to her daily workload. I felt so ill all the time, I didn't want to do anything, in fact at times I felt I didn't want to live. But down to earth as always she took it all in her stride.

At last late August arrived and in the heat of an unusually hot summer I went into labour.

'I just need to go to the loo, I'll be alright if I can go to the loo.'

That was my thinking about the pain in my lower back but mother knew the cause was the baby coming.

Thursday evening became Friday evening and then Saturday evening and no further nearer a delivery. By Sunday, the midwife, Nurse Davies, decided to send for the doctor. We had no telephone, neither did any other house in the Lane. The nearest public phone booth was quite a walk from the house and when the midwife arrived back she was fuming.

'He refuses to come,' she said, 'he says he is not on duty and therefore need not attend; it was his free time. Free time...' she blazed, 'he'll have more time than he knows what to do with when my report reaches the General Medical Council!'

Some twenty minutes later another doctor arrived and immediately said, 'hospital.' He would phone from the surgery for an ambulance which would be with us in about half an hour.

I had seemed to be dribbling water for the past couple of days and now had no clean knickers. Mother had washed my undies only one hour since and of course none were dry. I couldn't go to hospital not wearing knickers! Mother again had the problem solved. Reaching into the cupboard set in a recess alongside the fireplace she handed me a pair of large pink 'women's divideds', bloomers which reached from the boobs to below the knee.

'I can't go in those,' I protested.

'It's them or none at all.' Mother stood her ground.

'They won't stay up.' I held the voluminous garment in both hands watching them fall around my feet the moment I loosed them.

'Never mind,' mother reached into a drawer, 'this'll 'old 'em up.'

She handed me the largest safety pin I have ever seen. It would have served as a sign gracing any haberdasher store.

Dismay! It must have been written plain on my face but mother ignored it. Bundling me and my small lump into the brightly coloured knickers she wrapped the waist half way around again before securing them with the steel monstrosity.

Minutes later, me still feeling like a very unhappy, very trussed turkey, the ambulance arrived. Like as though it had to be, just as the two men came into the living room I had a really sharp pain. Leaning on a corner of the table for support it almost up ended. That was enough for the driver and his assistant. They had no intention of delivering a baby in the back of the ambulance. In two shakes Ralph and myself were on board and with bell clanging we were off. I learned later mother watched the vehicle pull away then collapsed in tears. Her daughter was in pain and she could do no more to help.

Arrived at West Bromwich Maternity Unit, the same drab and cream painted walls no different from the days when my mother had come to this place to give birth to her children, it was at that late hour and with, or at least it seemed, only one nurse on duty, so very like the asylum for the insane it had once been.

'Wait there.' A finger pointing Ralph to a chair the nurse whisked me away. Some time later she returned alone to where Ralph waited. Then with as much ceremony as if presenting the key to some city she handed him not a velvet cushion but my neatly folded clothes and there on the top were mother's pink bloomers and resting on them like some precious accolade the giant safety pin.

Monday morning eight o'clock my breech born 5lb 3oz baby made her debut into the world. Still lying on the delivery table, almost out of it after so many pain filled sleepless hours, the doctor in attendance asked me a question. Not having heard clearly and in no mood for talking right then I simply mumbled.

It was later that afternoon when one of the nurses asked 'why did I not want to keep my baby?'

Confused and not a little shocked I asked where had she got the idea I didn't want my child.

'You told Doctor Smith so after you were delivered. He asked did you want to keep the child and you said no.'

I couldn't wait for six o'clock. Visiting hours in nineteen fifty one were strictly regulated, no special amenity for new fathers.

Ralph was there on the dot. What was wrong? Was there something amiss with the baby? Listening while I blurted everything out he went in search of the ward sister telling her plainly baby Hutchinson would be coming home with her mother.

Returned to Dangerfield Lane he walked into the house and upstairs without a word. Poor mother; again she almost fainted. Her daughter had not survived childbirth. Back downstairs Ralph handed her a photograph of himself at six months old. 'There,' he said proudly, 'that's the image of the baby.'

CHAPTER NINE

After two weeks in bed and another week of pottering about the house regaining my 'sea legs' it was time to be 'churched.' This was a church service asking God to forgive my sin of bearing a child. This seemed a little hypocritical to me seeing the human race had been told to 'multiply and fill the earth...'

But without 'churching' I could not enter any shop nor visit anyone's house, so the arrangements made Ralph and I duly arrived at Moxley Church of All Saints the following Sunday afternoon. I remember nothing of that service, not the words of the priest neither those of the responses, something wiped the whole episode from my mind ... except for one thing. It was during a few moments of silent prayer. I was knelt, head bent low on my breast when against my ear the whispered voice of the priest said softly that 'next time you come be sure your head is completely covered or I will not perform the service!'

Had my simple hat been some sort of insult to God? How I wish I had then as I was to have years in the future, a degree in Biblical Studies, that priest would have gone home to the Rectory with his tail between his legs.

For the first time any of his daughters had known, father was ill. Sent home from Newman's Tube works with face and hands bright red and vastly swollen, mother saw him straight off to bed. As was the more usual in those days doctors were not called right away, there was an air of 'see how he is in the morning' still prevalent in the mind of older people despite that with the coming of social welfare, you did not have to have a doctor's fee in hand before daring to consult one.

Morning came and father was no better. Neither did he improve during the day and by early evening he was hallucinating. I couldn't be ruled by mother any longer, dad needed a doctor and I was going to call for one. A trip to the public phone at the top of the lane set the process in motion. A short time later the doctor arrived.

At the door of father's bedroom she came to a stop ordering the dark blue paper sugar bag Ralph had at mother's request fastened to the overhead light to shield father's eyes from the glare, be removed. The house boasted no such thing as a bedside lamp.

This done she examined the patient. The illness was poisoned Erysipelas, an acute infection of the skin and mucous membranes. He was running a high fever and must be nursed carefully. The following week was one of fear and very often tears from each of us caring for father, listening to him rambling on to people none of us could see. But eventually, thanks in no short measure to the doctor ... the turning point came and though he had to keep to his bed father began to improve.

In the Astbury household money had ever been in short supply but somehow mother had managed to feed her family of five daughters, her husband and herself; many times though she would go without, saying she had eaten earlier. This then proved good grounding for 'making do' but even making do doesn't work when no wage at all is coming in. This was the state of affairs once father's 'week in hand' (the first week of any employee's wage being kept in hand by the employer against such occurrence) had been paid to him. Things were becoming tight as a noose about the neck. I had my housekeeping from Ralph each Friday evening and what had been difficult for me managing on five pounds a week, now became even more worrying as it was stretched to cover mother's household as well.

Two weeks rolled into three until one morning walking to Darlaston for groceries, Lucy Harris, a friend and next door neighbour, nodded toward a small building which during the war had served as a learning centre for First Aid but was now the office for social welfare.

'Go on in,' she urged, 'tell them what's going on, they'll help.'

Of course they would help, why hadn't I gone to see them before now? This was the 'New World', the age of Government protection, a time where no citizen was left to struggle alone.

Or so my young mind thought.

Leaving Lucy to wait with pram and baby

I went inside. The man behind a large desk listened while I told of father's illness and so absence from work, that for three weeks my parents had received no money and now things were getting desperate.

'I see.' The man shuffled papers he had not set pen to. 'Tell your father to get a sub from his employer.'

'He has,' I replied, 'but his employer will not do that.'

'Hmm.' The man reshuffled the same batch of papers, 'In that case tell your father to sell his furniture.'

Hearing this my blood rose. My parents like so many more had lived through the hardship of the twenties slump, had experienced the bitterness of poverty, been ecstatic given a snared rabbit with which to feed a hungry family; then had followed the hardships of war with its food shortages but through all of this they had not suffered the indignity of selling off the few sticks of furniture they had struggled so hard to gather around them, and if I could help it they would not experience it now.

Having, quite heatedly, told this to the man behind the desk I watched him lay the papers on the desk, meticulously neaten every edge then slowly look up at me.

'And who are you?'

Hadn't I told him already? Where had he been while I spoke of my father?

Holding back my irritability I said quietly, 'I am Mister Astbury's daughter.'

'I see.' He stroked the top sheet of paper lovingly. 'And are you married?'

With my nod of yes he then asked was my husband in full time employment? Again I answered yes to which he snapped like a terrier, 'Then tell your husband to keep them!'

So this was the wonderful Social Welfare, the cradle to the grave care promised by the government. A promise judging by what transpired that morning that was like the proverbial pie crust ... easily broken.

My parents did not receive any help financial or otherwise.

Are there civil servants trained in what to say? Are they given certain phrases with which to answer people?

I ask this because in Nineteen Eighty Seven the exact words were said to my husband.

Still only a few months into marriage, mother in her wheelchair, me doing as much as I could to look after the family and home, I'd just pinned out a line full of washing. When I returned to the kitchen mother called me. Aunt Phoebe had arrived, she was sitting there in her best dress, best coat, all dolled up to the nines as she usually was. I had that same feeling that I had as a child, and I didn't find out my sister Ann had the same feeling until a few months gone, but the feeling was ... why can Aunt Phoebe always look so well off? So healthy and well dressed? Why can't our mom feel the same? Why can't she see that her family uses her the way they do? But she never said anything to them. As I pointed out in 'A Penny Dip' which spoke of a Black Country childhood – that was part of my childhood, watching my mom's brothers and sisters come only when they wanted something, only when they needed to be fed and then going back to sit in comfort for an hour or two in Aunt Phoebe's house before returning home.

I think I made myself promise very early in my life, one day ... one day if my mother hadn't got the emotional courage to tell them what they were doing to her, then somehow I would have my own back for her.

To return to this one particular Friday afternoon, I answered the call from the kitchen to see what it was she wanted.

'I want you to go up to the works,' she said.

Now the 'works' as us kids knew, was Newmans Tubes where father had worked since we came to live in Dangerfield Lane.

'You want me to go to the works?' I asked. 'What for mom, what do you want?'

'If you go an' stand by the big door yer dad'll see yer and 'e'll come an' give yer 'is wage packet.'

'His wage packet, what do you want that for? We're not going shopping until tomorrow.'

'No, no darlin',' she said, 'it ain't for me, it's for your Aunty Phoebe.'

My dad's wages were for Aunty Phoebe?

I said, 'Mom, how do you make that out?'

She said, 'She always comes of a Friday afternoon and borrows all your dad's wages but it'll be alright, 'er'll send 'em back at teatime, 'er always sends 'em back.'

I asked, 'Always? Well who gets them up to now?'

Mom looked a bit sheepish saying, 'Me, I usually fetch 'em but since my leg's been amputated Mrs. Norton round the corner's brought 'em for me, but she can't bring 'em this week. She's not very well so she's not going up.'

Oh I thought so this is how Aunt Phoebe goes up the town on a Friday afternoon when there isn't a soul in the street, or in the streets around apart from Mrs. Noone, the local money lender, who would have a penny left at this time. The only ones to fetch their husband's wages in the afternoon, round about two o'clock were the ones who would fetch the clothes out of the pawn which had been pawned on Monday morning, to get the men's shoes and suits brushed and ready for them to go out on a Friday evening. Apart from that there was nobody in the town except Aunt Phoebe, who went round like some belated film star opening her purse very wide whenever she made a purchase so that people could see the folded pound notes contained within.

My dad's folded pound notes!

No. This wasn't going to be for me.

I said, 'Mom, I'm very sorry, you don't need me to go for anything for yourself at the moment.' I turned to Aunt Phoebe and said, 'If you want the money Aunt Phoebe I'm afraid you're going to have to fetch it yourself, because I'm not fetching it for you.'

She looked very shocked but there was nothing she could do as she could see I was quite adamant. I was not going to fetch my dad's money so she could swan around the town showing off to her heart's content.

My sisters, well from Ann downwards, when they knew what I'd done, showed indifference, perhaps it was me, perhaps I was a little bit 'harder' than them, but I still don't regret it!

Some twelve months into marriage and feeling the financial screw tighten more every month, I thought whenever I saw a particular bargain I couldn't believe it. Half a dozen pairs of men's interlock underpants for thirty shillings, one pound fifty in today's money. Half a dozen pairs for that! Normally it would cost me two pounds forty something. I thought thirty shillings a lot to pay out of what I had but then again it's a very good saving. Eventually I bought the pack of underwear, got it home still very pleased with the bargain until I broke the seal ready to wash them before being worn.

It was then, when I opened one pair that I saw the logo P D enclosed in an oval with a crown over the top. Oh my goodness I thought, what have I bought? Prison underwear! But never mind it would go very nicely with the convict haircut he got himself every month – at least he would match top and 'bottom'!

125

CHAPTER TEN

The days went on. Me trundling from one to another, trying keep mother's household head above water as well as my own. But at last father was well enough to return to work and things seemed to get back to normal. That was, for a very short time, for Ann had been visiting Hilda in the North East, showing her her new son Paul, came back and was shortly followed by I don't know whether to call him a boyfriend or admirer at the time, but whilst she'd been at Hilda's house, she'd met John Rewcastle, and he like Ralph and Bill before him, had travelled back down to the Midlands following Ann home.

What was it about my family that seemed to attract men from the North East? Three out of five of mother's daughters marrying a Geordie. Whatever it was Ann and John Rewcastle seemed to be genuinely in love. There was only one thing for it, Ann and her husband were to separate. This they did, seemingly a few days after Ann returned from the North East. But where to live? Once again, mom and dad stepped into the breach. They came to live with us. So Ann, John Rewcastle, and Ann's son Paul, three years old, moved in with mother. Luckily there was one empty bedroom, very small, but at least it held a bed and a cot for Paul. The strange thing to me is, Ann paid mother one pound fifty pence a week for their keep, which was fair enough, but that made the slice of my payment towards the household accounts even deeper. It cut even further into my five pounds, because the three of them were being fed, obviously, and my contribution didn't alter. Mom had one pound fifty more but I had nothing. Not that I minded, it's just that, well you can't help but think about these things can you? I was struggling very, very much as it was to feed and clothe three people on five pounds a week. It might have sounded a lot at that time, but it wasn't. With one pound fifty out of that for your rent, and then food and all the rest of it, and trying to clothe a young baby, my own little girl, I was gathering more grey hairs than enough.

John Rewcastle apparently, working at Lloyds, Darlaston, had told mom he was on an even smaller wage than Ralph was getting. Whatever the truth of it was, I don't really know. All I do know is, mother said 'right, one pound fifty will do.' Now, this much I've never told to a living soul, not in all the years it's been with me. But early one morning, Lucy, the next door neighbour, who spent more time in mother's house than she did in her own, came in whilst I was cleaning the front room, the living room. And on the hearth was a very small, tightly folded, wad of paper – like a narrow ribbon of paper. 'Well I don't know what it is', I said. And Lucy said, 'well open it and look.' So I opened it and looked and it still didn't make sense to me. I hadn't seen anything like that before. I'd never seen, or even asked to see Ralph's wage slip which is what this piece of paper proved to be. A wage slip. But not dad's, not Ralph's, but John Rewcastle's. And instead of the four pounds he told mother he was earning at Stewarts & Lloyds, he was earning fifteen pounds! I've never forgotten that. I never shared it with mother; I never shared it with Ann. I hope, if and when, my sister reads this or hears it, she won't be too upset. It wasn't your fault, my darling.

Not very long after that, John somehow heard of a room to let in Birtley where he came from, and Ann, and he and baby Paul moved back to the North East.

Things it seemed, were back to normal, but not for very long. Mother received a letter to say Hilda had contracted Rheumatic Fever and was in bed and quite ill. Naturally she was on the next train up to Newcastle upon Tyne, and I was left to look after dad, and the household. When you think about it, for a young girl, eighteen, it seemed as though one burden was piling on top of another. But nevertheless, we dealt with it. Mother stayed for a few weeks, and then obviously with dad missing her, and us missing her as well, she came home, but Hilda still needed help, and it seemed that once more, it was to be myself who was to go there and do it. So, with baby Lindsey in tow, I went to Birtley to live with Hilda, to look after her, for as long as it took. It took, I think, almost two years, and in that time mother and I took it in turns to look after her. The last of my turns lasted so long that Ralph came up in the end to fetch me home.

There were other sisters, of course there were, but none seemed to volunteer to go to look after Hilda. So like I said, it was mom and myself took turns until eventually Hilda was allowed out of bed and well on the way to recovery.

That one little upset was quickly followed by another. Mother wasn't very good on her legs. As I probably told you, she was born crippled. Her right arm wouldn't lift of its own accord, though that hand had all of its movement and strength. The left leg was badly twisted and kept in what we called 'leg irons'. This then began to give her quite a lot of trouble and for two afternoons a week she was taken to Walsall Hospital for them to keep an eye on it and see what was happening. Then one day she came home with it in plaster, just her big toe sticking out of the plaster. The afternoon, I recall, was quite hot and sunny and mother complained of the heat in her foot. 'Oooh,' she kept saying, 'Oooh my big toe is hot. Eeh wench if only I could cool it.' Well she couldn't have said anything better than 'could I cool it.' Lindsey, sitting on a stool at mother's feet, with an ice cream cornet in her hand promptly plonked the ice cream cornet over the big toe and said, 'is you better now grandma?'

The ice cream incident might have cooled things down for the moment, but not for very long. Mother seemed to get gradually worse; her weight dropped to seven stone and, though I never understood this, the doctors said it was the leg draining the life and energy out of mother and it would be far better for it to be amputated, which it was, below the knee. That put mother in a wheelchair. Now, little things she may have been able to help me with before, were now a thing of the past. She was stuck in that wheelchair and she could do nothing except advise which, to me, has always proved to be excellent. The advice given me by my mom has lasted me a lifetime. But the problem was, although mother was in a wheelchair, Phoebe didn't seem to recognise the fact. She still brought Olwen, who was by that time about, what, two years old to be minded, and during the school holidays, Andrew, five or six years old, for mother to care for whilst she was at work.

Well, in a wheelchair, it had already been proved, mother couldn't care for herself, so there was another burden landed on my shoulders. It wasn't my house; I couldn't say, 'Phoeb, you can't leave them here.' That wasn't up to me, but while the children were there, they obviously had to be looked after, given a meal, washed and kept clean, kept interested during the day, and with a small child of my own, this didn't prove an easy task. It seems that my life has been one round of one problem after another, but at that time, believe me, I was just about ready to pack the whole thing in!

This wasn't what I'd thought marriage to be. I didn't think it was going to be one round of hardship, one thing after another, but I never mentioned it to Ralph; as my mother said when I discussed with her how short the housekeeping money was, 'you haven't got to say anythin' to 'im wench, 'e goes out and earns the money, it's up to yoh to keep 'im 'appy and to see that 'e 'as no problems.'

To see that he has no problems. That stayed with me all my life and only now do I realise what a mistake it was not to discuss those things with Ralph. Not to let him know how hard things were for me; if he didn't know, he couldn't do anything.

CHAPTER ELEVEN

Phoebe, who lived in a little old Victorian house on King's Hill, rented, was given a new house, just built, on the Millfield Estate. Quite a nice house; large airy rooms, very nice. Mother was taken by me, pushed all the way to the Millfield in a wooden chair that must have been old in Victorian times! It had been lent to us by the Welfare group somehow, and it was an old wooden thing, with wooden wheels, rickety, straight back, it really was an antique. But somehow or other, I managed to get her to see Phoebe's house on the Millfield. That was it! Mother wanted one! And what mother wanted, mother got! She applied for, and was granted, a house, number 24 Pembroke Road. Semi detached, adapted apparently for a wheelchair – this was an absolute ruse – in fact it was an absolute lie! Mother still had to get up the stairs; it hadn't been adapted for a wheelchair. The downstairs consisted of a tiny, tiny room 9 feet by eleven – I had to measure it for carpet, so I know what width it was – with a fireplace. Next to that was a lovely, large, square airy room with no fireplace and no means of keeping it warm. So, in the long cold winter months, all of us were squashed in this tiny, tiny, nine by eleven feet living room.

The worst part of it was, mother could get to the bottom of the stairs by her wheelchair but the toilet was upstairs. What design was this for a semi invalid? The only thing she could do was go upstairs on her bottom pushing herself up with one leg, and then, once at the top on the landing, during the day I had to somehow drag her along to the toilet and hoist her on. Now she was rapidly putting weight on by this time, and it really was a feat of arms for me. But we managed. But that wasn't the only drawback in taking this house, it was a disaster from the beginning. For father who formerly had only a few minutes walk from his work down Dangerfield Lane to number fifty one, which was a nice, easy access to and from work for him, now he had to walk up quite a steep hill and quite a distance to catch a bus that only ran once an hour. If that was gone, if he missed it, then he missed his work.

Ralph also, was now a long way away from Rubery Owen which was the other side of Darlaston, a long bicycle ride. But no matter, we were there, and we had to make the best of it.

Some time after moving, mother was fitted with an artificial limb. This was a bit of a struggle for her, but bless her, she tried her best. At the hospital they measured her for some shoes. Now mother had never worn anything in her life from earliest childhood up until that moment except these surgical shoes. The irons up her legs and the boot itself reaching almost to her knee, and the other shoe also surgically designed. Anyway, full of excitement, she told us she was to have some new shoes, and she'd chosen them herself. These were brown leather. She didn't know when they'd be delivered, but each day she watched for the post man evermore excited. The shoes didn't come. Christmas was almost here. Mom and dad were going to visit Hilda for the Christmas break. Before they went, mom said to me, 'If me shoes come wench, you will send 'em to me wow ya?' Of course I would.

A couple of days after they'd gone, the said shoes arrived. They were, as she'd said, brown leather, nicely polished, plain but quite acceptable, like a good country walking shoe. So, I put them in the post and sent them off to her. And Hilda told me later, it was the best Christmas present mother had ever had. She'd put them on, one on the artificial foot, one on her own foot and she just sat there gazing at the shoes, like Cinderella gone to the ball.

CHAPTER TWELVE

At times, during the day, I would think about my life. It seemed no different from that of a Victorian kitchen drudge, working from the minute of getting up in the morning, 'til going to bed at night. What had I done to myself? In that one moment of uncontrolled, I'd given away my life. Yes I loved Ralph and Lindsey; I loved my parents, but why did my life have to turn out the way it had? Every night I would pray that the next day things might improve. That perhaps there might be a little extra money from somewhere. But every day this proved to be a fallacy. There was no extra money. Life didn't seem to be getting any better.

Then I was pregnant with my second child. This time there were no few months where mother could take over, and I could sit by just watching things go on. There wasn't as much sickness, but then again there wasn't the comfort of mother. She was in her wheelchair; there was nothing she could do at all. I then realised I just had to get on with it. As I remember a few of the worst months, it was absolutely awful. But eventually on 21st March I went into labour. This time the child was going to be born in my mother's house on the Millfield. That was fine, the midwife came, I was in the front room with the midwife and Ralph sat in the living room with mom and dad. She told me later he sat at the table, he put his head on his arms and he never moved or made a sound until the baby was born. But by that time, that the baby was born, he'd gone to work anyway. There was no having a day off; there was no paternity leave for fathers in that day. And my own dad, of course, had gone to work as well.

When he came home in the evening, he came into the front room where the baby was in the cot by the side of the bed, and he said, 'Ma wench, I'm gonna wet that babby's 'ead'. He wasn't going to let anything stop him. It must have been about half past ten – eleven o'clock the same night when father came home. He'd obviously been more than friendly with the pint glass and he stood at the bottom of the bed and he said, 'Cock,' which is a word of love in my part of the Midlands; it's a very, very friendly greeting bordering on a loving thing, 'Cock,' he said looking at the cot at the bottom of the bed, 'I've bought that babby a present, it's cummin' tomorra, I've bought 'er a cockabulldog!' Oh my God, I thought, now what? Not something else, please God not something else! All the next day I lay in that bed in dread. Fortunately the cockabulldog never materialised.

The new baby, a girl, we named Kim and she seemed to cry day and night, day and night for no reason whatsoever. But I had noticed because my own milk failed, I had to put her on formula. Every time I fed her formula, she would cry out in pain, screw her little legs up tight against her tummy obviously in pain. I mentioned this to the doctor, I mentioned it to the social worker, but nothing seemed to be done, and it was gradually drawing me, having no sleep night and day. I knew dad and Ralph had to go to work in the morning, so when she cried at night I would walk the room with her trying to keep her quiet.

This went on for some two or three months until one Saturday I was in Wednesbury town and the pram was outside the chemist shop as I was waiting to be served, when she started to cry again. I said to Lindsey who was standing by me, 'go and rock

138

the pram darlin' and see if you can keep Kim quiet.' Anyway she did as she was told, but the crying didn't stop. It got so bad that the chemist came out from his little kiosk at the back of the shop and asked whose child was crying. I told him it was mine. The man very kindly listened to all I had to say and then he said to me, 'Take my advice, my love, switch her from the food you are giving her, to one that's called Truefood. It's very expensive I know, at seven shillings a tin,' at that point I nearly fainted, but I managed to listen to him, 'but I've been to the factory where it's made, and it's broken down and rolled, broken down and rolled, time and time again, until it's the nearest thing to mother's milk that it's possible to get.'

I took the man's advice and bought a tin there and then and from that moment on, the crying stopped and Kim seemed to improve, growing healthily. What it turned out to have been was she had a sort of milk allergy and the same thing showed in her own little boy when he was born many years later.

As usual, life seemed to tumble from one crisis to the next. Soon it was time for Lindsey to start school; she was five years old. Now any mother who has taken her child to school for the first day will know what I mean when you talk about the pain when you see that child taken away from you. Taken into the classroom, the door shut; you're no longer wanted. That happened to me; I cried all the way home, and I watched the clock all day until it would be quarter to three; time to go and fetch her from school, it was a good half an hour's walk. I got there, the school playground was deserted except for one woman, Mrs. Joan Smith, who lived a little way from the school just down the street. She must have realised what had happened and taken Lindsey into her care – Lindsey by the way was heartbroken, she must have thought her mother had forsaken her – when I turned up. The clock apparently had been slow, causing me to turn up at school when all the other children had gone home.

I couldn't thank Joan Smith enough and she turned out to be a very, very good friend for many, many years after that. When Lindsey didn't like school dinners, she said, 'let her come to me, I'm feeding five, another one wow mek no difference.' And so she did. Joan, if ever you read this, I thank you with all my heart.

Growing up couldn't have been very easy for Lindsey, she was, and is, THE most dedicated follower of fashion! She used to watch the girlie magazines, which incidentally Olwen got, I couldn't afford to buy such things, and whenever anything was new, obviously like all other kids her age, she wanted one. Well money being what it was the only way she could get anything was when it was home made. I knitted all their woollies, even their winter socks, and made dresses, petticoats, the only thing I didn't make were their knickers and shoes. These, of course, were always a little more difficult to come by. Lindsey, of course, took exception to home made clothes; she didn't like it at all. But it was either that or do without. Then fetching her from school one day, my own shoes with heels so worn down that I was walking on the body of the shoe – no money to get any more from anywhere else. Imagine my feelings when I saw other women look at my feet. But, there was nothing I could do about it.

Then, one afternoon as always, as I came in from school, mom was sitting there in her wheelchair and she said, "ere ma wench, ya go out in the mornin' and ya spend that on them babbies.' It was a Provident cheque. Now apparently as I could see how this worked, the caller came every week and you paid him a certain amount of money for what you'd borrowed, say a £10 cheque and you paid it off weekly. Well mother had had a £10 cheque and she gave it to me saying, 'there you are ma wench, that's for yoh, yoh'm good to me, yoh'm good to ya daddy, doh think we doh appreciate it.' I couldn't have thanked anybody any more. I felt so uplifted. I bought the children some underclothes like I said, and I managed to keep enough to buy myself a pair of shoes. The next day I went to fetch Lindsey from school it seemed I walked on clouds of air.

CHAPTER THIRTEEN

I, of course, like so many other young couples, was on the Council housing list for a council house. I would go down regularly, at least once every two or three weeks to see where I stood in the queue but always it seemed I stood at the bottom. Now, with mother being as crippled as she was, artificial limb as well as her other disability, she was eligible for a bungalow. One morning this wonderful letter came from the council, there was a bungalow empty on the Friar Park Estate. Now this was quite a walk from the Millfield, but having taken Lindsey to school, Kim sat on mother's lap in that antique wooden wheelchair, that rattled and rolled every step of the way, I pushed her all the way down to the Friar Park Estate. We found the said bungalow and my heart stopped.

Yes, more than anything else in the world I wanted a home of my own, but when I looked at that house, there was no way on God's earth my mother was going to live there. The toilet was broken, the tiles on the floors were smashed, the ceilings were hanging down to the floor, it was in the most dilapidated, terrible state; in fact, in my opinion, it should have been flattened! The Friar Park Estate at that time didn't have a very good reputation anyway, it was termed 'a rough area'. Combining that with the bungalow I made up my mind there and then, supposing I lived in lodgings for the rest of my life, my mother was *not* going to have that bungalow.

I explained it to her as I wheeled her all the way back to the Millfield and I think she felt as I did, a little relieved that she didn't have to go and live on the Friar Park Estate.

It was a couple of years after that I think,

I was upstairs making the beds and I looked through the bedroom window and just across the green – a big area of green space had been left on the Millfield Estate in the part where we lived – there had been four or five bungalows built across there some time before. There was a funeral cortège lined up in front of one of the bungalows. I found out later that day that there had been only a lady living there and she unfortunately had passed away. Now, it might seem not quite the thing to do, but chance when it offers itself has to be grabbed with both hands, that much at least I had learned. So off I went to the Council offices explaining what I'd seen and what had happened, and they said leave it with us and I was dismissed.

A couple of weeks later we had a visitor, it was the woman from the housing department. She came in, sat down in mother's living room, made herself comfortable and during the course of conversation she asked why the bungalow at Friar Park had been turned down. I explained, and I said, although I know the house would have been perfectly acceptable by the time it was turned over to my mother, she couldn't get around at all on her own, and it was much too far for me to walk two or three times a day to look after her. So unfortunately we had to say no to that particular property.

'Oh I see,' she said. Then she looked through the window down the garden which was lawned on both sides edged round with gladioli and all sorts of flowers and she said, 'who's done the garden?'

And I said, 'Well I have, me and my husband together, we've done the garden.'

She said, 'In that case, if you've done the garden, you deserve the house.'

And so it happened mother was given the bungalow just yards across from that house and I was given occupancy of mother's three bedroomed house.

It was a dream come true in many ways, the only thing that marred it for me was the tiny, tiny squeezed in space that had a fireplace and the lovely open room that hadn't. So some months after having it turned over to me, I asked at the housing department could someone come and have a look which this man did, and I said could I have these two rooms joined into one to make it a more acceptable use of space?

He studied the ceiling for a few minutes and said, 'No, no you can't, the beams were put in the other way round meaning you can't knock the fireplace wall down.'

Not long ago, I was talking to a neighbour who still lives next door to 24 Pembroke Road, which has since gone to quite a young man who bought the property from the council and she said the very first thing he did was to have that fireplace wall knocked down. But it seems it wasn't to be that way for me and Fate proved it was going to be a very different kettle of fish from then on.

Mom and dad hadn't been out together for a very long time, mom in her rickety wheelchair not wanting to be paraded through the streets. But this one evening she said yes, she would go with dad for a drink. They would go to the Millfields Public house which avoided having to push the wheelchair up a sharp hill. So, both ready, off they went.

About half past ten dad arrives home again a little bit too jolly with the pint glass. He liked his drink but he rarely went over the edge, however this night he'd had enough and he was tired.

He comes in on his own, flops down on the settee and Ralph said, 'Where's mom?'

No answer. Ralph shook dad saying, 'Dad, dad where's mom?'

Dad replied, 'Er's 'ere ay 'er cock?'

Well obviously she wasn't there.

Ralph said, 'You took her with you, where's mom?'

But father was off with the fairies, he was fast asleep. Ralph dashed out of the door, ran all the way to the pub and when he got there the whole building was in darkness. The streets were dark and empty and mom was sitting in her wheelchair up against the pub wall.

'What happened?' he asked.

'I don't know,' she replied, 'we were gonna come away when he said he had to go back to go to the loo, and 'e must 'ave gone out of a different door and forgot all about me.' Which, of course, was what had happened.

It was a long time before she went out with him again.

We laugh and giggle about it now but at the time it was no giggling matter and the next day father really got it in the neck from mom.

Father was a regular visitor coming across the green – you'd hear my two girls whoop with joy, 'Granddad, granddad' and they'd run to meet him.

One Sunday I remember he came across, Lindsey had gone with her cousin Olwen, Phoebe's daughter, they'd gone off somewhere together, leaving Kim alone with me. 'Never mind cock,' said my dad to Kim, 'come on I'm gonna tek yoh up the cut, we'm gonna catch ya some Jack Bannacks.' These were tiny little tiddler like fish. So, complete with jam jar, string tied round its neck for a handle and a net on the end of a stick they both went off towards the canal. Some time later they came back and I heard my father say, 'Now put your fish round the back in the shade and give 'em some clean water.' He then came in to talk to Ralph and myself, after a cup of tea and a chat he went home to mother.

Next thing I know Kim's in floods of tears saying, 'my fish won't swim.'

'Your fish won't swim?' Strange, so I went to look at the jar and the fish were all lying at the bottom like a little black cloud.

'Well what have you done?' I asked her.

'Granddad said put some clean water in,' she cried.

'So, did you put clean water in?'

'Yes, I boiled the kettle and I poured it in the jar and now them all dead!'

Poor little fish... Kim never did grow up to be a doctor!

CHAPTER FOURTEEN

Dad had had really serious bronchitis and he hadn't gone back to work after the Christmas holiday. This one morning I thought dad's at home with mom, she's alright for the time being, so I can do a few extra jobs in my own home before I run across the green and go to the bungalow where my parents lived, so I thought. A few minutes later dad comes rushing in, 'Cock, cock, y'll 'ave to come and 'elp me wi' yer mom, I cor get 'er into bed.' I dropped everything and we both ran back to the bungalow. Mother was sprawled on the floor at the side of the bed and no matter how we tried to lift her she was a 'dead weight'; she had put a lot of weight on by that time. She'd given up trying to walk on her artificial limb which caused her a lot of pain so naturally the more she sat in the wheelchair the more weight she put on.

We both tried to lift her into bed and couldn't manage. So I thought I'll go out into the street, surely someone will be passing who could come and help us get her back into bed. But it turned out to be one of those days where there's nobody else in the world except you. The streets were empty, they were silent, there was no help to be got. I went back into the house and somehow between us we got mother into bed.

She couldn't speak, she couldn't move; I sent for the doctor. He came right away, she'd had another stroke. He took me into the sitting room and said, 'Be careful what you say because your mother, although she can't speak, she can hear everything that's going on around her. Whatever you do, don't distress her.'

Now, as the day went on, things seemed to get a little worse. Ann and Hilda still lived in the North East – should I send for them as I sent for Hilda when mother had her first stroke? It had turned out not to be as bad as we thought so it was rather a long journey which, then, seemed for nothing. Yet if I didn't send for them and anything happened to mom, I'd be in hot water. So, I sent for them. I had to telephone a public house nearby as they didn't have a telephone at the time and word was sent to Hilda. That evening when Bill came from work he drove them both down through the night to Wednesbury.

By the time they got here it was too late. But just before they arrived mother, who hadn't spoken all day, Phoebe was one side of the bed, I was the other side of the bed, both kneeling down, I had mother in my arms, Phoebe was holding her hand and was saying, 'it's me birthday tomorra mom, it's me birthday the tenth, doh leave me on me birthday.' Just as she said that the doctor walked into the bedroom. I took my arms away from mother whilst he examined her and of course he told us the worst had happened, he was very sorry but she'd passed over.

When Hilda and Ann arrived, like I said, it was already much too late. But Hilda went into the bedroom and when she came out her face was a study.

'She's been knocked about!' she said angrily.

I looked at her dumb-struck. Mother had been knocked about? By whom? There's not one of us would let a feather brush against her let alone hurt her in any way.

I said, 'What do you mean she's been knocked about?'

'Well go and have a look at her.'

So I went in and there were huge purple bruises under the skin, on her face, down her neck and arms and her chest. I was horrified – it did look as though she'd been knocked about. But as the doctor explained to me later, this was the cause of I think he called it subcutaneous bleeding. Bleeding underneath the skin she'd had a very, very serious brain haemorrhage. And it was that, that had killed her.

For the next two years father walked about like a man lost. I honestly think I did my best for him. He kept his bungalow. By this time I'd moved to another house about the same distance from the bungalow but on the other side of the street. I looked after him as well as I could; I never wanted him to come in to a dark house that seemed empty as it really was. So in the winter, I'd go over when it was time for him to appear from work, I'd put all the lights on, I'd put the gas poker to the fire, put his slippers by the side of the fireplace and he'd have a hot meal waiting for him when he came in.

In the summer, the same thing, a meal always ready. It was as much as I could do and I did it willingly.

About two years after mother died, again in January, the 21st, father comes over to my house. I'd lit his fire as usual, left everything ready for him; I even remember the meal I left him – it was beef stew with dumplings – and I knew it was a favourite of his. He came into the kitchen where I was setting the table for the children's tea and he said, ''Ave you got a sixpence for the gas love, the gas has gone out under me fire and it ain't quite lit.'

I said 'yes Dad,' I remember I had two sixpences in my change that day and dropped them into my pocket for exactly that reason, keeping them for dad's gas meter. So I went into the hall to fetch the sixpences from my coat pocket and when I came back Lindsey was on my dad's back, he had Kim in his arms at the front swinging her round and round, laughing and enjoying themselves, all three of them acting like kids. He put Lindsey down and he turned to me and he takes me in his arms and he said, 'Y'know cock, y've took the place of yoh mother. I thank you.' Then he went home.

It wouldn't be a couple of hours after that when I was upstairs doing something and Ralph called up the stairs, 'Marg, it's your dad, he's collapsed.' I didn't need wings on my feet, they didn't even touch the ground.

You see my dad liked company, he loved company, and he found some of his best company in the local pub, so he'd finished his tea, washed and changed and gone for his usual evening to the pub. When I got there, Phoeb and me seemed to race in at the same time, and dad was lying on the floor. His eyes were still half open and you could see the laughter in them. He had the most amazing blue eyes did my dad, they always seemed to twinkle, and although he was dead they were no different; they were twinkling, they were laughing.

The barman looked at me and he said, 'He come in as usual love, he ordered his pint, I turned away to get his change from the till, and when I looked back he'd gone. It was then I looked over the counter and saw him there on the floor.' Of course the 999 call was made and the medics came to take him away. Phoebe and I went with him, Ralph followed in the car to bring us back. At the hospital it was just said DOA, dead on arrival. But the doctor that looked at him was kind enough to turn to me and say, 'My dear, he wouldn't have felt a thing. It would be like a door had slammed in his face.' It was certainly a door that slammed in my face, and when it opened again it was to open onto an entirely different world.

CHAPTER FIFTEEN

The children were both at school, my parents were no longer alive and I had more free time on my hands than I'd ever had. I got myself a short, part time job at a firm called T&P Products at West Bromwich. They were very friendly people, nice women to work with. They understood I'd had a couple of short sharp shocks the way things had gone with my parents and I was glad of their company. I forget which crisis was on in the world at that time whether it was the Cuban crisis with President Kennedy in America, I can't quite remember, but I know there was something quite serious on that affected us. I had a very, very small portable radio and I took it with me into the work-shop and stood it on the bench. It was turned on very low; there was no mechanical machinery in operation so it couldn't provide any danger by taking people's attention away from what they were doing; putting small pieces of electrical things together.

The boss walked in and without even

looking at me walked past the bench and said, 'Turn that off.' I thought that was rather rude but it was his prerogative, his factory, if he wanted it turned off he could have it turned off, but he could have at least said please. As this was going on through my mind, he'd reached one end of the shop and turned round to come back the other way. As he got to me he said, 'I thought I told you to turn that off.' This was too much for me; my nerves were in a raw state and nobody, especially him, was going to get away with anything.

I put down the piece of work I had in my hand, switched the radio off, looked at him and said, 'Yes, you did tell me to turn it off, now allow me to tell you something. You are one of the most rude men it's ever been my misfortune to come across, and as for your job – you know where you can put that and I hope, for the next twelve months at least, you walk as though you have severe piles!' Then I walked out of the factory.

It wasn't until I was walking down the street and was almost home I thought to myself ... good God what have you done now? That little money you were earning there was doing quite a good job and now look what you've done, you and your big mouth. I'd always been a bit hot tempered as Ralph had learned during the years I told you about, we'd done wrong and I wasn't going to let anything stop punishing both of us for that, so more or less every day we had words about something. But instead of going into the house as I'd intended, I walked down to Wednesbury and on the way back I decided to come home on the bus. Along the inside of the bus was an advert, the local colleges were taking on new students. It was the time for joining the college. I thought and thought about it when I got home.

I had my home which I loved, I had my kids who I adored, I had my husband who I adored. A husband who seemed to think I shouldn't want anything except just that. But I did, and I realised all through the years of marriage there had been something missing in my life. I'd never quite been able to put my finger on what it was but I knew there was something missing. Reading that advert helped me to realise what it was. I needed something other than the home to interest me, to broaden my mind, to broaden my horizons if you like.

So, deciding that attack was the best form of defence I waited for him to come from work. By this time, we'd acquired a very ancient car, a real old banger but it did the job. I only ever waited for him to come from work in the garden if there was anything wrong with the children and they needed to go to the doctor, so he wouldn't put the car away in the garage and then have to get it out again. So when he saw me standing there he immediately said, 'What's wrong? Is it the kids?'

'No,' I said, 'I'm going out.'

Well, to say that he was deflated – attack really had proved a success – he did look deflated. I got in the car and he said, 'Where are you going?'

'I said I'm going to Wednesbury College of Commerce.'

'What are you going there for?'

'I'm going to see what they've got on offer. I want to do something else besides cleaning and cooking. I want to do something that will satisfy me.'

This didn't seem to please 'His Majesty'. He drove me to the college and just before I got out of the car he said, 'Look, I'll just ask you one thing, as long as you're in the house when the kids go to school and when they come back from school I don't care what you sign up for, I don't care what you do.'

Fair enough. I went into the college and

told them quite frankly what I didn't want, and in the end I decided on English and Maths. I never got further than fractions at school; they frightened the life out of me. I'd wet my pants every time she wrote fractions on the board! Nevertheless I thought in for a penny, in for a pound, English which I'd always enjoyed and Maths which I'd always feared.

It was quite an experience. The first morning the new college term started I turned up at nine o'clock. The classroom I was in was a group of sheds added to the side of the main building to take the overspill. The lecturer in charge was Mr. Scrimshaw, a really, really nice understanding man. I sat, deliberately, on the front row. I must have thought I'm nearer the door here, I can make an escape.

The first shock of the day was when the students walked in. None of them were a day over seventeen and they all looked at me as though I was Methuselah's granny! I was thirty three years old by the way. In they piled, some two dozen of them, all going for the very back of the room, all giggling, all pointing – I can't explain how I felt. I was cringing inside but at the same time I was determined not to be robbed of this one chance. I'd stick it out, somehow or other I'd stick it out.

This went on for a few weeks until one morning, in they came as usual, one young girl detaching herself from the group and coming to sit by me on the front row, and she said, 'Do you mind if I sit by you, Mrs. Hutchinson?'

My answer was, 'I'd be very glad' if she'd sit by me. From that moment on I became one of the group. All these young people so friendly, making sure I was included in all they did – come with us, sit on the grass, eat your sandwiches, have a cup of coffee in the refectory – wherever they went I was included. Life to me was great, I was enjoying what I was doing. Yes sure Maths was hard, I didn't know you could have less than nought, apparently you could, even though the lecturer in charge of Maths, and there was only me in that one group, Mr. Kilner showed his distaste in every shape and form. No, he didn't teach me how to do anything, he put work on the board and sat reading a book while I tried to plough my way through it. If I asked him a question, he snorted. But, even he wasn't going to drive me away.

Then one morning as I sat as usual, alone

before the other young students came into the room, Mr. Scrimshaw came and sat on the desk opposite me and he told me the college were thinking of running a course of some eight months for mature students. It was a course series of 'O' levels and if these mature students could get the 'O' levels on what they called the paper, which meant sitting one a week or whatever, and passed each one, then they would have an interview for the Teachers Training College in Wolverhampton with a view to entering the teaching profession.

Yes please, this was me! Definitely. I went to see the college principal. Yes, he said he thought perhaps I should go to see the Principal and Vice Principal at Wolverhampton Teachers Training College. An interview was arranged, and I went to it. Talking more or less about my main interest, Archaeology, and at that time, the Dead Sea Scrolls had just been found, and were on exhibition in London for the first time. I could not conceal my excitement at going to see them.

At the end of the interview the Principal said, 'Well, I've known you for what, for half an hour, but I would definitely, definitely say that you were teacher training material.' So I was given a place.

I came back from Wolverhampton on cloud nine, if I could get those five 'O' levels then I had the chance of becoming a teacher. There were some eight mature students including myself signed on for the eight month course, the subjects being:

English Language
English Literature
Geography
History and,
R. I.

There were some of the happiest times I had known, we laughed and giggled like children. Then came the crunch. Each afternoon for a week a new 'O' level paper. When I learned I had all five I couldn't help but jig. Mr. Scrimshaw invited us all to coffee in the refectory and seemed genuinely pleased for us. Mr. Kilner on the other hand said sourly, 'I wouldn't trust them to teach idiots.'

Vote of no confidence number two.

At fifteen years old the school Head Mistress had said I would 'never do any good,' I 'would never get anywhere'. Now at thirty three another member of the education profession was saying I couldn't be trusted to teach idiots. I really would like to know what they thought now of that erstwhile student who after her name can write the letters, B.A. L.C.P. B.Phil. T.E.G.L.

A student who went on after 25 years of teaching to become a very successful author!

I went into Teacher Training College and two years into the course a man came to speak to the students and he'd come from, I think we would term them today mentally challenged. If we would leave college with a two year degree and go into teaching the mentally challenged, he could guarantee us a post right away. Now, the friend I'd teamed up with from the very beginning, from going into Wednesbury college, Pauline Sillitoe, she said she was going to do it, and was I going to come? I said no. That wasn't my choice at all. I would prefer to finish the three year degree course and go into the normal classroom. Which I did.

It was my last eight weeks of teaching practice I was placed at Lyng Primary School in West Bromwich. The Head Master Mr. Dodd showed me to the classroom, and the class teacher who was to be in charge of me. I was supposed to be taking the class for short periods of time during the day whilst the class teacher was there to observe and to make sure everything went okay. I saw that class teacher that first morning, who never even showed me the register, and for the eight weeks after that he never once turned up in my classroom.

I did all that a class teacher had to do even though I was unqualified, I even had to do playground duty twice a week which was illegal but a blind eye was turned to it. At the end of the eight weeks, everything was over and done and all I had to do from then on was to keep my fingers crossed and hope that I would be offered a teaching post somewhere. I did get a teaching post. Apparently, as he told me later, Mr. Dodd had gone to the Education Offices and asked for me in person to be assigned to his staff. I was assigned to his staff and I remained there at Lyng Junior School as it then became known, for twenty five years.

My eight weeks helped prepare me for things to come later in life. Things that might not have been got through so easily had, let's say for instance, this not happened.

As I told you before the teacher in charge of the class I was given put in an appearance the first morning I got there and for the rest of the eight weeks I never saw him. But this didn't mean that any of the children's lessons could be allowed to go by. One of these lessons included swimming. The children had to be walked up through the town quite a distance to the town baths and they would go two classes together. One class at the swimming baths while the other class was at the library, and then they would change over, the other class would have the baths and the other the library.

I went this one morning, I was told I would have to go with them whether I was qualified or not, and the teacher from the class next door took his class so at least there was one qualified member of staff there, with seventy two children. The shock came when my children had finished their swimming lesson; they had already been in the library and I marched them back into the library to join up with Mr. Wye for the return home and he said to me, 'I'm not going back to school.' When I asked the reason he said, 'I've had a 'phone call from my wife,' she was a chemist somewhere, 'and she says I have Yellow Fever and I've to go straight home, go to bed and send for the doctor.'

What was I going to do ... stranded, a student, no qualifications, seventy two children to get back to school? What did I do? If I 'phoned the school was there anyone else there to come up and help? I thought the best thing to do perhaps was to get them back to school on my own and take the consequences once I got there. So, fortunately, they were very well behaved kids, they were quite good, and we walked back down to school without anything untoward happening.

Mr. Dodd, the Head Master, stood on the steps of the main entrance as he always did. 'Well,' he said, 'how have you got on?'

'Everything was alright.'

So he said, 'Where's Mr. Wye?'

When I told him what had happened, he just shrugged his shoulders and walked into his office. Now what did I do? I had seventy two children so who would have the other thirty six? Where would I send them? Nobody said a word ... nothing. The only thing I could do was take Mr. Wye's children into my classroom. We filled every chair there was to be filled, the others having to sit on the floor. There was an hour before the dinner time break and I had to manage seventy two kids for an hour before the bell went for dinner. Fortunately that too went without mishap.

The very fact that I was left stranded like that helped in a way because much, much later in my career I took two classes of children, fifty odd, down to Earl's Court for the Royal Military Tattoo. The coach was organised by the Head Master, Mr. Dodd – an old friend of his who owned the coach firm said he would take us. I should have known something was wrong when he said, 'Oh we won't go the motorway route, we'll go Oxford way, it's much prettier.' But it was a lot longer round and with fifty odd children on board it might have been a disaster. However, the disaster waited until after the show.

We were on the way home, no other qualified teacher just me, and fortunately – or unfortunately for Ralph really who was unemployed at that time and I wanted someone with me who could take the boys to visit the toilets which I obviously couldn't do. So Ralph came with me. We got to London and the coach driver said, 'I don't know where Earl's Court is.' We drove round and round the streets getting no nearer Earl's Court from what we could see and Ralph said, 'Stop here, stop on the corner and I'll go into the newsagents and get an A to Z.'

Whilst he was in the newsagents a police motor cyclist pulled up, gets on the steps of the coach and shouts, 'Who's in charge here?'

I said, 'I am.'

He said, 'Well get this coach off the street. Her Majesty is expected in a few minutes'.

Now I wasn't very pleased, so I said to him, 'Well if you can tell me where to put the coach, I'll see that it's put there.'

'Get it off the streets,' he said and disappeared.

So much for that. Ralph gets on with the A to Z book, shows the driver the way, talks him through it, and we eventually arrive at Earl's Court, quite late.

Everyone had to be searched before they could go into the auditorium and when it got to me, I opened my bag. There was a police woman on duty and a male police sergeant. She said, 'You can't go into the show.'

I said, 'What do you mean?'

She said, 'Well you can't go in, Her Majesty's arrived.'

By this time, I'd had just about enough, and perhaps a better thought slipped my mind because I said, 'Bugger the Queen! I've got fifty kids here and I don't care who's in the auditorium!'

And with that the police sergeant fell back across the table laughing saying, 'Oh I like that, I do like that,' he said. Well whether he liked it or he didn't I marched the kids into the auditorium to their seats, and I, for one, don't think for a minute that Her Majesty would have wanted any of those children kept out of that show. It wasn't their fault that they were late, it wasn't their fault they arrived after she did.

Now with the stress of getting in to see the Tattoo in the first place, you would have thought that would have taught me a valuable lesson. Don't go any more, and don't take fifty-odd kids with you if you do! But, like all things, it was quickly forgotten.

The next year when the Tattoo came round, I took fifty children and down we went to London. The same coach firm that took us before but this time, under a different headmaster. Everything went fine until we were part way back to school, and the coach broke down completely. I didn't know what to do, but luckily again Ralph was with me. He took the boys to one part of a field for a wee, I took the girls behind some old buildings on another part of the field while the coach man worked at the engine.

Hour after hour passed; I telephoned a hospital, which I think was a mental hospital where I felt like going in and staying in! At the gate I asked if I could telephone school to inform them of what was occurring. I rang school and when I said 'hospital' the headmaster almost had a fit. I reassured him no one was hurt, all of the children were fine, it was the coach that was in a bad way.

We finally ... finally arrived back at school at one o'clock the following morning, and from the crowd I heard one of the mothers say, 'I dow know what her's thinkin' on, fancy keepin' the kids out 'til this hour of the mornin'.' If only I could have given her my answer. She would have opened her eyes, I tell you!

CHAPTER SIXTEEN

Coming home from secondary school one day, Lindsey handed me a letter. The school were taking a trip to Switzerland.

'Oh mom, can I go? Can I go?'

You can imagine the excitement. Now although we were a little bit better off financially by this time, scraping together enough money to pay her fare to Switzerland and to give her some spending money, it had to be decided against one other thing – any fancy, shop bought clothes. I had always made their clothes and Lindsey had always resented it, she just didn't like it at all. But, she was given the choice – she could go, we could just about manage it, but she would have to have any clothes she wanted made by myself. She opted for Switzerland. That was fine, she was delighted.

How strange when you think back how much she detested having to wear clothes that I'd made for her, and yet when it was her turn to get married, who did she come to, to make her wedding gown? Yes, you guessed it. Mom.

That wasn't to be for some years yet. In the meantime we had the situation of a teenager growing up. Talk about walking on eggshells! I understand everything they say about that. My problem came in the form of a young man called Malcolm. Lindsey had found herself a boyfriend. Now for some reason I could not take to this lad, no matter how I tried. I just didn't like him and it must have shown. Anyway, one Christmas we were all going to stay with Hilda, and Lindsey asked if she could stay at Malcolm's. His mom had asked her if she could stay for the Christmas holiday.

'Well yes,' I said, 'if the woman had been kind enough to ask, then yes you can stay.'

She wanted to know if she could borrow the put-u-up bed. So she was lent the bed and all the things she needed and off we went. When we came back from holiday, there was no Lindsey, but there was a letter there and it was from Malcolm's mom. What kind of a woman did I think I was putting a daughter out on the streets at Christmas? Locking the house and leaving her alone in the streets to look after herself. This was not a woman that she would very much like to meet. So that was me. The mother who'd agreed to let her stay behind for a holiday, it seemed, had turned her out. I think this hurt Ralph emotionally more than I've ever seen him hurt before. It took him months and months to forgive her.

Gradually the situation eased and she would call in on a Saturday afternoon for five minutes while the Malcolm 'problem' stayed outside.

'I'm sorry,' I said to her, 'I just can't have him in, and I don't intend to have him in my house. If you want to go with him, that's fair enough, there isn't very much I can do about it.'

This went on for what must have been at least a year and in all that time Ralph never spoke a word to her. Although I tried to talk him round – no, he was having none of it. He'd been hurt much too deeply.

Then one evening I arrived from school at the usual time around five o'clock.

'I want to come home, I want to come home.'

So, what else could I do?

'Bring the bed and your things back, and you can come home.'

The problem didn't ease there, although she promised there would be no more scenes with Malcolm ... there was. In the end, I delivered an ultimatum. I wasn't going to have her coming home at two and three o'clock in the morning after being with that lad all that time. So she could make up her mind, either she lived by my rules as far as that was concerned, or else she must find herself a decent lodging.

It still took some time after that, but eventually Malcolm faded from the picture. Not so much the problem, that transferred itself to a young man called Chris. He also thought it was alright to think it was okay for her to get back at two o'clock, until one morning – it would be about three o'clock, Kim came from her bedroom into mine. She was shouting and frightened. When I asked her what was the matter she said there was something outside trying to get in at the window. Well naturally I rushed right into her bedroom and there, in the garden, was Lindsey.

The next morning I went off to school as usual, and when I came back, I gave her again the ultimatum. Either alter your ways, or alter your lodgings. Either come in at a decent time, eleven or twelve o'clock at night or you find somewhere where you can come and go as you please. It didn't alter that much and the only reprieve I got was when she said she and Chris were going to get married. That to me, was like the bell at the end of a fight, and like I say, who did she come to, to make her wedding gown ... me!

One evening she came from work with a big bundle of tulle that looked as though it needed a damn good wash. When I asked what it was, she said it was a second hand wedding dress she'd bought. I looked at it and decided to keep quiet, it was nothing to do with me, it was her wedding, if she wanted a second hand wedding gown that looked positively grey with dirt, that was her prerogative.

'Tell me what colour you want Kim to wear as bridesmaid and I'll make the dress for her.' So we settled on a russet amber silk taffeta top and a russet brown velvet skirt. Using the pattern I'd made myself – I always made my own patterns from brown paper and newspaper – so I showed Kim the pattern.

'Yes,' she said, 'that's quite nice.'

So, I made the dress, and one evening she was trying it on for last minute alterations when Lindsey came in.

She took one look at the dress and said, 'Mom, can I have one of those?'

I said, 'Well you've already got your wedding dress.'

'Yes,' she said, 'but I'd like that one instead.'

We bought the satin, we bought the pearl beads and mom set to work again making the wedding gown in the same design except there were three separate tiers for the back and each one was covered with pearls and hooked onto the waistline of the wedding dress itself. Though I say as shouldn't, I was really, really pleased with the effect – and so was Lindsey.

At fifteen, Kim was awarded a scholarship at Gordonstoun. She and I went together to look at the school; a heck of a journey such a long, long way. However, she seemed quite pleased with it and at the start of the new school term things began as usual. But before long I was getting very tearful 'phone calls. Mom, I want to come home, mom I don't like it, mom I want to come home. I could understand that, she was in a strange place with strange people; first time in her life she'd been separated for any length of time from home, but thinking I was acting in her very best interests I tried my best to ignore these 'phone calls.

Then one day, at lunch time at school, the children came, 'there's a 'phone call for you Mrs. Hutchinson.' This call was from a Dr. Smith introducing himself as coming from Aberdeen. He'd been called to Gordonstoun to look at Kim and decided she needed an appendectomy. He thought I should be there with her.

The first headmaster I worked for, Mr. Dodd, how on earth he heard what was happening I don't know, but he walked into the secretary's office where I was taking the call and when I put the 'phone down he said, 'I think you'd better go Meg.' He was the only one in my life who ever called me Meg and now I'm known as Meg Hutchinson.

I rang Ralph at work, told him what had happened and I got the first train to

Gordonstoun. It took me seventeen hours to get there, changing train after train, and all the time this worry on my mind, what was really going on?

I eventually reached the hospital and a Sister showed me to a screened off cubicle where Kim was lying. As she allowed me inside and closed the curtain behind me I heard her say, 'A love such as this, you don't see that very often.' When I looked at my daughter her face was covered in boil like eruptions. I hadn't seen anything quite like that before.

A while later a woman doctor came to see me saying she didn't agree with her colleague that Kim needed an appendectomy. She said, 'As far as I'm concerned, there's nothing physically wrong with your daughter, it's all in the mind. It's what we call psychosomatic; the mind forces the body what it's refusing to do. Kim's body was refusing, apparently, to give way to what the mind was saying. You haven't got appendicitis you're too unhappy.'

She talked with me for a long time saying 'I want you to bear in mind Mrs. Hutchinson, what's happened once, will happen again and the next time your daughter could be anywhere. She could be on a railway station, she could even be in a different country somewhere; I want you to think very carefully about leaving her behind.' She was as good as saying really, I think, that it would be better if we took Kim home, which eventually we had to do.

I thought perhaps it would damage her education, but since then she's finished up as a PhD in Maths and Science so perhaps I didn't do too badly after all.

Much the same thing happened when, quite a few years later, it was Kim's turn to be married. We looked and looked at wedding gowns and wedding patterns all over the place and she couldn't find anything at all that she wanted. She's always had strange ideas has that one and this one was proving to be a real strange idea! I asked her to make a sketch of what she wanted, so she did.

I said, 'If you can't find what you want, while you're looking, what if I buy the material and have a go at making one, if you like it fair enough, if you don't it hasn't cost you anything. Shall we do that?'

'Yes,' she said.

Off we went, bought all this beautiful, beautiful white figured heavy silk. I made it more or less along the lines she'd drawn, and now she wanted an over bodice, three quarter sleeve, open down the front like a little jacket and she wanted lace. But no ordinary lace, Oh no, she wanted antique lace! Now where the heck, especially on my budget, would I find antique lace? That was what she wanted, so we decided to go to Birmingham 'Rag' market. If you can't get anything there, you might as well forget the whole thing because the world and its brother go to the 'Rag' market, to sell, to buy – anything.

It was while we were rummaging about on one stall that I found a blouse and again, it was grey with dirt.

I said to Kim, 'That's a nice, pretty looking bit of lace, very delicate, that's what you want.'

We bought the blouse, took it home and washed it, and it came up beautifully white and clean. I cut it up and made the bodice she wanted with the three quarter sleeves. Fine, that all turned out very well.

The next problem was Matthew. This was Lindsey's son, three or four years old by this time. Kim didn't want him dressed in a page boy's uniform, she didn't want a little sailor attendant, or a little soldier, so what the heck did she want him dressed in? She didn't know.

I suggested that seeing as all the adult men were going to be dressed in grey morning suits, why not have Matthew dressed exactly like them in miniature.

'That's fine,' she said, 'but where can I get that from?'

Well, as you've guessed – out comes the brown paper and the pencils and I made myself a paper pattern of a grey frock coat. Fortunately from the same 'Rag' market I'd bought a bolt of grey velvet. The coat turned out to be perfect, and with grey trousers, black patent shoes, a pair of little silk gloves of mine that were dyed grey, and a neck tie to go with it. Everything was fine, but what did I do about the top hat? He had to have a top hat. We had a new headmaster by that time, and he was very nimble with his fingers and I asked him about it.

'Oh,' he said, 'if I cut you the pattern out can you cover it in velvet?'

So I did. He helped me by cutting the design out, including the outer edge, which I covered in grey velvet.

On the day, Matthew was dressed exactly like the adults, and though I say it as shouldn't, I was very proud of that little bit of handiwork.

CHAPTER SEVENTEEN

Three years at teacher training college filled, and myself now a qualified teacher I would have thought that that sense of unfulfilment that I'd felt all those years before would have been satisfied. But no, it wasn't. I still seemed to want more and more learning. I first took an evening course at the local college leading to a diploma in social services. Then, still not satisfied I took a two year course in Biblical Studies leading to the L.C.P., Licentiate of the College of Preceptors. Now I would have dearly loved to have taken it that one stage further but £60 for reading the finished thesis on top of the normal fee for the course, proved just too much. So I never did become a Fellow of the College of Preceptors.

Though I'd completed my eight weeks of training at Lyng, and thought probably never to see that school again, I did in fact spend the next 25 years there. All the time I was there, I would take a course in one thing or another never, never seeming to be satisfied. There was always something else I wanted to do, something else I could prove to myself I could do. That's how it was for the whole 25 years until it came to retirement.

We retired to a tiny cottage in Shropshire, quite isolated. We came to live here in the August and by Christmas, having had such a busy life, I was tearing my hair out wondering what I could do to keep myself sane! I had left two tea chests in the conservatory which had not been unpacked from the August – shows how lazy I am! I decided to unpack these and dispose of whatever was in them.

Prior to moving in the August, whilst emptying cupboards and getting ready for the move, I filled three huge black plastic waste bags with stories that I'd written, long, short, detective, romance – you name it, I'd written it – and they had all got thrown into these bags, which the bin men had taken away.

At the bottom of one tea chest I came across a manuscript. The pages were yellow, it must have been at least twelve years old; I was just about to carry it to the dustbin when Ralph came in from the garage, saw the papers in my hand and asked, 'What are you doing with those?' I told him I was going to throw them into the dustbin. 'Well before you do that,' he said, 'why don't you ask someone to look at them?' Now who on earth would want to look at my scribblings? They were not good enough for anybody to look at, it had just been something that had satisfied myself whilst on holiday and various moments in my life when I had five minutes to spare, when I would go to my favourite pastime of writing.

Once it was out and down on paper, I never gave it another thought. It either got thrown away there and then or pushed into the cupboard to be got rid of at a later date. However, he insisted, so I contacted an agent in London and asked would she be kind enough to look at my work. Yes, she agreed, would I send something to her? A couple of weeks later I received a telephone call from this lady asking could I go down to London to see her? I was so excited, so excited!

We went down, Ralph and I; he took himself off for a couple of hours while she and I sat and talked. The outcome was she was very interested in the story I had sent and she said, 'Are you doing anything else?' I answered that I was, out of sheer boredom I had begun to write another story. I outlined it for her and she said, 'Get it done as quickly as you can and let me have it.' I needed no better prod than that! Within a month it was done. I sent it down to her, and within three weeks I had a telephone call to say she had sold both these stories to Hodder & Stoughton and they'd given her a contract for four more, sight unseen.

I was very naive at this and had never done it before; I'd had no dealings whatsoever with publishers and agents, so I asked, 'I'm sorry to seem so ignorant but what does sight unseen mean?'

She said, 'You write them, and they'll publish them.'

From then on I've written and Hodder, very, very grateful on my part, have accepted every one. Thanks to all of that goes to my agent, Ms. Judith Murdoch. I'll never be able to thank her enough for what she did for me.

CHAPTER EIGHTEEN

You might have thought my not being able to countenance spending £60 plus on another exam to get a Fellowship of the College of Preceptors that I would have forgotten all about learning any more. However, when the opportunity arose whilst I was teaching of secondment to Birmingham University for a B. Phil., and the chance was offered to me, I jumped at it.

With yet another new headmaster Mr. Swindell, calling me into his office, he was all for it, he wanted me to go. 'But,' he said, 'you won't be able to come back here, you won't be able to take up your teaching post here again.'

'Why not?' I asked.

'Well you won't be able to,' he said.

Then I reminded him I was taking secondment, I wasn't resigning my post at school. It made no difference, he was still adamant, 'You won't be able to come back here.'

I thought the best thing to do was to contact my Union representative; I couldn't

185

afford to give up my teaching job. I telephoned the Rep, and put it to him.

He said, 'I've never heard anything so daft in all my life. How long has he been a headmaster? Where did he get his information from?'

The outcome was that I took the chance and I went to Birmingham University for a twelve month secondment to get a B. Phil., in Psychology of Childhood.

At the same time, Kim, my second daughter, was at Aston University doing her degree in Maths and Science. The days came for the Awards Ceremonies, Kim's being one day, mine the next day.

Things were a little easier on the financial side for the family but it still didn't mean Ralph could have two half days off in succession. So we were agreed, Kim's Award Ceremony must see both of us there. We both attended and the next day it was mine. My sister Joan came with me and witnessed me being given my degree for which I'd worked hard, and for which I'm still very, very proud.

CHAPTER NINETEEN

Short Back and Sighs ... a strange title to give to any piece of work but though the short back ended some forty years ago – it's been that long since Ralph went to a barber as one day in one of my usual tantrums, I vowed and declared I could cut his hair better than the one who was doing it, leaving him looking like a prisoner.

'Right,' he said, 'next time if you can do any better, you do it.' So I did. And I've been doing it ever since.

One evening, whilst talking about doing his hair, we began to talk about family in general. While he was talking he mentioned a Joseph Hutchinson.

'Who,' I asked, 'is Joseph?'

'He's my brother.'

I said, 'I didn't know you had a brother named Joseph.'

'Yes,' he said.

Ralph's sister, Amelia, was the eldest, Bill was the next eldest who married my sister Hilda, then came Joseph, and Ralph about six or seven years old at the time.

I asked, 'Why is it I've never met Joseph?' And then the story came out. Talk about surprises!

Joseph apparently, for a fourteen or fifteen year old, was full of beans. From what I can gather I don't think he was a tearaway but Amelia did. She was in charge of the family, the mother of the family as their own mother had died giving birth to a little girl younger than Ralph.

Ralph was only one year old when his mother died. There had been confusion as to Ralph's age at this time, but looking at the birth certificate shows his age to be one year when this little girl, Kathleen, had been born.

This was a lot to ask Amelia to look after, all the grown ups and Ralph at only twelve months old and another little baby girl, it was too much for her. So Kathleen went to live with an aunt.

However, it was Joseph I was interested in.

'What happened to Joseph?' I asked.

'He was put away.'

'What do you mean...' I looked at Ralph, 'put away?'

'He didn't much like being told what to do all the time he was in the house.'

Melie was one for rather bossing them about, and Joseph had lost his temper and thrown something at Melie. Ralph at about seven years old at this time was unable to remember what was thrown. When his father came home from work at the pit, Amelia said, 'It's either him or me, I'm not putting up with it any more.' Joseph, poor soul, was 'put away' ... he was put in an institution and from that day until the day I was talking to Ralph no one had seen or heard of him again.

By this time, Ralph and I both agreed it was perhaps a little late to start looking. We had no way of knowing whether he was still alive or not. It wasn't so very easy in those days to trace where people were but whenever I think about that young man I feel very, very sorry for him, and I don't usually raise it any more in conversation.

The haircuts were finished from then on as I did them myself, but the Sighs were not finished. I still felt as I had as a young woman. I'd hurt my parents, I'd let them down, I'd betrayed them and for that reason I should be punished. I was still picking faults with every little thing, making as many arguments as I could with Ralph. All I can say is thank

God he had the patience of the Biblical Job.

This one night we were talking and I told him the way I felt; he just looked at me and said, 'Do you really think your mother didn't know? Do you really think she had no idea? You should give your mother more credit than that, she certainly had a lot more sense than you give her credit for.'

'Why?' I asked.

'Look at it like this, she wouldn't have had me in the same town let alone the same house as you had she thought for one minute that I absolutely didn't adore the very ground you walked on. She could see, Marg, I loved you, I've always loved you and she could see that no matter what happened in life I would still love you. And *that* was why she let me stay at your house. Your mum was expecting what happened. If you remember, she didn't seem at all surprised because she knew, one way or the other, we would always be together and I'd never, ever let you go.'

That was a little bit of good advice from Ralph. It stopped all the arguments; I could at last after all those sixty odd years show how much I really, really loved him.

So now, not only have the short backs ended, but the sighs have ended too.

The publishers hope that this book has given you enjoyable reading. Large Print Books are especially designed to be as easy to see and hold as possible. If you wish a complete list of our books please ask at your local library or write directly to:

Magna Large Print Books
Magna House, Long Preston,
Skipton, North Yorkshire.
BD23 4ND

This Large Print Book, for people
who cannot read normal print,
is published under the auspices of

THE ULVERSCROFT FOUNDATION